THE
NEW, COMPREHENSIVE, AND IMPARTIAL
HISTORY OF
Pirates
FROM A VERY EARLY PERIOD OF
AUTHENTIC INFORMATION

EDITED BY HARRY KNILL

ILLUSTRATED BY GREGORY IRONS

With many particular Circumstances worthy of Notice in the ANNALS of PIRACY, including:

BATTLES, ATTACKS, REPULSES, RAVAGES, REPRISALS, CONQUESTS, DEFEATS, PLOTS, BARBARITIES, SEA-FIGHTS, MASSACRES, ASSASSINATIONS, EXECUTIONS, SURRENDERS, CONSPIRACIES, ASSOCIATIONS, STORMS, SHIPWRECKS, TEMPESTS, MORTALITIES, COLONIES, LAWS, HURRICANES, COMMERCE, JUSTICE, VOYAGES.

On the cover is
Capt. Bartho. Roberts
by Major Neary

Copyright © 1985 by

ISBN 0-88388-027-X

Bellerophon Books, 36 Anacapa Street, Santa Barbara, Ca 93101

Send a stamped, long envelope for our swashbuckling catalog.

JULIUS CAESAR & the PIRATES

In the times of *Marius* and *Sylla*, *Rome* was in her greatest strength when certain pirates broke out from *Cilicia*, a country of *Asia Minor*, situated on the coast of the *Mediterranean* betwixt *Syria* on the east, and *Armenia* on the west. This beginning was mean and inconsiderable, having but two or three vessels and a few men with which they cruised about the *Greek Islands*, taking such ships as were very ill armed or weakly defended. However, by the taking of many prizes, they soon increased in wealth and power. The first action of theirs which made a noise, was the taking of *Julius Caesar*, who was as yet a youth, and who being obliged to fly from the cruelties of *Sylla*, who sought his life, went into *Bithinia*, and sojourned a while with *Nicomedes*, King of that country. In his return back by sea, he was met with, and taken, by some of these pirates near the island of *Pharmacusa*. These pirates had a barbarous custom of tying their prisoners back to back and throwing them into the sea. But, supposing *Caesar* to be some person of a high rank, because of his purple robes, and the number of his attendants, they thought it would be more for their profit to preserve him, in hopes of receiving a great sum for his ransom. Therefore they told him he should have his liberty, provided he would pay them twenty talents, which they judg'd to be a very high demand, in our money, over $75,000. He smiled, and of his own accord promised them fifty talents.*They were both pleased, and surpriz'd at his answer, and consented that several of his attendants should go by his direction and raise the money. And he was left among these ruffians with no more than three attendants. He passed eight and thirty days, and seemed so little concerned or afraid, that often when he went to sleep, he used to charge them not to make a noise, threat'ning, if they disturbed him, to hang them all. He also play'd at dice with them, and sometimes wrote verses and dialogues, which he used to repeat, and also cause them to repeat, and if they did not praise and admire he would call them beasts and barbarians, telling them he would crucify them. They took all these as the sallies of a juvenile humor, and were rather diverted, than displeased at them.

At length his attendants return'd with his ransom, which he paid, and was discharged. He sail'd for the port of *Miletum*, where, as soon as he was arriv'd, he us'd all his art and industry in fitting out a squadron of ships, which he equipp'd and arm'd at his own charges. And sailing in quest of the pirates, he surpriz'd them as they lay at anchor among the islands, and took those who had taken him before, with some others. The money he found upon them he made prize of, to reimburse his charges, and he carry'd the men to *Pergamus* or *Troy*, and there secured them in prison. In the mean time, he apply'd himself to *Junius*, then *Governor* of *Asia*, to whom it belonged to judge and determine of the punishment of these men. But *Junius* finding there was no money to be had, answered *Caesar*, that he would think, at his leisure, what was to be done with those prisoners. *Caesar* took his leave of him, returned back to *Pergamus*, and commanded that the prisoners should be brought out and executed. And thus he gave them that punishment in earnest, which he had often threatened them with in jest.

No vessel can peep forth, but 'tis as soon taken as seen.

Even more than the terror, the odious ostentation of these pirates aroused indignation. They had gilded masts and purple sails and silvered oars, as if they reveled in their iniquity and preened themselves on it. Livy

* A talent equaled 390,000 grs. of silver, which today would be $3,753.14, and multiplied by 50, $187,657.

3

TURGEIS THE VIKING

The *Vikings* were sea farers who plundered and robbed. They went *í viking*—like the pirates of 1720 went *a-pirating*. Under *a man of genius, Turgeis,* a prince from *Vestfold* in *Norway,* they came with a great red fleet in 831 or 832 to the north of *Ireland,* and with them came *Ota* (or *Aud*), the priestess-prophetess (*Vala*) wife of *Turgeis.* This woman soon sat upon the high altar of the monastery of *Clonmacnoise,* having chased the monks out, and the people came then one by one to consult her as an oracle. She travelled about with her magical arts in a splendid chariot, and the days of her coming were festivals.

They were *Norse Lochlannaigh,* from the lochs (the *Norwegian* fjords) of the *Vestfold* around *Oslo* fjord. This name also meant sea-demons, giants, as well as pirates. The endless wars in *Ireland* between the kings of *Ulster* and *Munster* helped *Turgeis* the *Gaill* (stranger) to conquer the *Gaedhill* (native), with the support of one *Irish* tribe annoying another. He set up a new *Norse* kingdom in *Conn's Half,* or *Northern Ireland,* and with *great sea-cast floods of foreigners Turgeis* set about taking the rest of the island.

He easily sailed up *Ireland's* inland waters with three fleets of light and shallow longships, and set up his capital on *Loch Ri,* half way up the *Shannon River.* Then sixty-five of his ships appeared at *Ath-Cliath,* the forerunner of *Dublin* (*Dubh-linn* or *Black-pool*), which was first taken in 838. The *Vikings* built a fort there, which became a great port and *Ireland's* capital.

Al-Ghazal (the *Gaselle*) was the chief diplomat (and a poet) of the *Amir of Cordova.* In 845 he journeyed to a *Viking* court, considered to have been *Turgeis'* in *Ireland.* A description of his embassy was discovered in 1937 in the library of the mosque of *al-Karawiyin* at *Fez. Al-Ghazal* sailed on this journey *between waves like mountains,* and he *looked death in the eye.* But he arrived finally and met the king, *Turgeis,* who sat in great pomp. *Peace, O king,* said the elegant *Al Ghazal,* not impressed, until he met *Queen Ota. Why does he stare at me so? Ota* asked an interpreter. *Is it because he finds me very beautiful, or the opposite? Al Ghazal* the diplomat replied, *I did not believe there was so beautiful a spectacle in the world.* Soon they were more than friends, and their dealings together became notorious. *Al Ghazal's* companions warned him to see less of the queen, but *Ota* laughed: *We do not have jealousy in our religion,* she said. *A woman remains with her husband only as long as it pleases her, and leaves him when it doesn't. Before the religion of* Rome, Viking *women refused no man.*

Turgeis, the terror of the *Irish* church, appointed himself abbot of *Armagh,* the patrimony of *St. Patrick. Ota* continued her pagan worship at *Clonmacnoise*—they were setting up the *Scandinavian* gods in place of *Irish* Christianity. But *Conn's Half* was also the home of the most warlike and powerful of all the *Irish* clans, the *Hy-Njall,* or *O'Neil.* By 845 *Njall Caille* recovered some of his old power, and beat the fierce *Vikings* in a battle. And then a southern *O'Neil,* one *Malachy (Maelsechlainn),* got hold of our *Viking. Turgeis* being enamored of the daughter of king *Malachy,* it was arranged that she should receive him at a banquet, in an island on *Loch Uair,* where she appeared, surrounded by 15 beardless youths in female attire. They carried arms, however, concealed under their garments, and when *Turgeis,* who had also 15 attendants, advanced to embrace them, they took him prisoner and drowned him in a lake.

Here is part of a gorgeous helmet worn by an ancient Nordic seafarer. You can wear this helmet, one of several, printed in gold and silver, in MAGNIFICENT HELMETS, at your store or write: Bellerophon Books, 36 Anacapa St., Santa Barbara CA 93101. We also have VIKING SHIPS to cut out.

EUSTACE the MONK

I shall tell you of a monk
  who came from near the sea.
This monk went to *Toledo* where
  he learned necromancy.

Soon there was no man in *France*
  knew magic half so well.
He made it hot for people, and
  the *Devil* taught him spells.

The *Devil* taught him many ways
  to ruin and burn the folks.
He learned 1,000 conjurings
  and spells with which to hoax.

An old sword he could demonstrate
  and make it turn and clap.
From here to *Santiago* no one
  knew more *Zodiac.*

A *chimera* he conjured up
  to scare the cloistered fools,
& when he thought he'd learned enough,
  he left the *Devil's school.*

That Devil told him that he'd live
  as long as he'd do ill;
with kings & counts he'd war at length,
  and in the sea be killed.

When asked about a tavern bill,
  poor *Eustace* could not pay.
The mistress swore she would collect,
  he hexed her straightaway.

Her skirts flew high above her waist,
  her casks of wine marched out
& pulled their spigots out themselves,
  and wine flowed roundabout.

The townsfolk hurried after him,
  this myst'ry they would probe.
He cast a hex before their doors
  which caused them to disrobe.

Soon *Eustace* tossed a magic seed,
  no wine was lost at all;
the women dressed themselves again,
  and home went one and all.

When *Eustace* had become a monk,
  quite dev'lish things did he;
when the monks would do their prayers,
  soon cursing they would be.

The *Abbot* said as follows:
  If tomorrow you're not beat,
the Devil *grab me by the throat!*
  So *Eustace* did this feat:

He conjured up an ancient witch,
  all stooped and old and mean.
In Mary's name, the *Abbot* cried,
  It is the Devil's *dream.*

The *King of England* hired the monk,
  with ships he went to sea,
out to the *Isle of Guernsey* where
  he fought quite fearlessly.

Eustace swung a mighty axe
  and cut more than one neck.
Many helmets he would nick
  whilst bloodying the deck.

His prowess brought him victory;
  he said, *Let's watch them flee!*
Before the fray was o'er & done,
  the corpses filled the sea.

Eustace sailed to anch'rage where
  the *Seine* flows to the sea.
He sailed up to a bridge where stood
  Cadoc of Normandy.

The monk sat shaving on the bridge,
  half hidden by a frock.
What will you do to Eustace *when*
  he's caught? he asked *Cadoc.*

Cadoc replied *The* King of France
  will singe his pantaloon.
Then *Eustace* said *Lend me your cape,*
  you'll see us catch him soon.

Eustace bade him follow—into
  quicksand fell *Cadoc,*
whose yelps brought help from 1 hayraker
  born of peasant stock.

But *Cadoc* thought him evil and
  protested all he could.
Behold, laughed *Eustace, how maligned*
  are those who would do good!

'Tis I, by name, Eustace the Monk,
  who's brought you to this funk.
Now wallow here, go on, you're free,
  be happy you've not sunk.

Eustace raised his sails up high,
  a ship he did espy.
It was so richly laden, *Eustace*
  boarded this ship nigh.

Eustace went to *England* (for it
  did deserve the man),
His palace was so grand it brought
  the *King's* own reprimand.

Then to *Boulogne* next he sailed and
  by the by he learned,
that *England's King,* quite out of spite,
  had had his daughter burned.

Time went by and *Eustace* held
  his grudge until at last,
a fleet of 20 *English* ships
  was sighted from the mast.

The monk attacked the *English,*
  and he made great homicide.
He broke some arms and heads but was
  assailed on every side.

The *English* tried with all their might,
  their axes fell like rain.
But *Eustace* quite enjoyed the fight,
  the *English* could not gain.

The enemy then threw some lime,
  a cloud of dust arose.
The pots exploded with the slime,
  which stung them in the nose.

They now no longer were so fierce,
  the cinders filled their eyes.
The wind conspired to slow their flight,
  the *English* breached their sides.

The enemy indeed had won,
  our monk was very dead.
They left him with no allies, and in fact,
  without a head.

Our *Eustace* thought that sorcery
  would fill his life with song.
But hist'ry shows that evil men
  cannot live very long.

From the 13th-century *Wistasse le Moine,* never before Englished. It starts out: *Del moigne briement vous dirai . . .*
il avoit a Toulete este. See also the English Historical Review, 1912, *The Battle of Sandwich and Eustace the Monk.*

Sir ANDREW BARTON *the famous* SCOTS PIRATE

As itt beffell in midsumer-time,
    When burds singe sweetlye on every tree,
Our noble king, King Henery the Eighth,
    Over the river of Thames past hee.

Hee was no sooner over the river,
    Downe in a fforrest to take the ayre,
But eighty merchants of London cittye
    Came kneeling before King Henery there.

'O yee are welcome, rich merchants,
    Good saylers, welcome unto me!'
They swore by the rood they were saylers good,
    But rich merchants they cold not bee.

'To Ffrance nor Fflanders dare we nott passe,
    Nor Burdeaux voyage wee dare not ffare,
And all for a ffalse robber that lyes on the seas,
    And robbs us of our merchants-ware.'

King Henery was stout, and he turned him about,
    And swore by the Lord that was mickle of might,
'I thoght he had not been in the world throughout
    That durst have wrought England such unright.'

But ever they sighed, and said, alas!
    Unto King Harry this answere againe:
'He is a proud Scott that will robb us all
    If wee were twenty shipps and hee but one.'

The king looket over his left shoulder,
    Amongst his lords and barrons soe ffree:
'Have I never lord in all my realme
    Will ffeitch yond traitor unto mee?'

'Yes, that dare I!' says my lord Chareles Howard,
    Neere to the king wheras hee did stand;
'If that Your Grace will give me leave,
    My selfe wilbe the only man.'

When my lord Haward saw Sir Andrew loose,
    Lord! in his hart that hee was ffaine:
'Strike on your drummes! spread out your ancyents!
    Sound out your trumpetts! sound out amaine!'

'Fight on, my men!' sais Sir Andrew Bartton;
    'Weate, howsoever this geere will sway,
Itt is my lord Admirall of England
    Is come to seeke mee on the sea.'

But when hee saw his sisters sonne slaine,
    Lord! in his heart hee was not well:
'Goe ffeitch me downe my armour of prove,
    For I will to the topcastle my-selfe.

But Sir Andrew hee was shott then;
    He was hit upon he mark;
Under the spole of his right arme
    Smote was Sir Andrew quite throw the hart.

Yett ffrom the tree hee wold not start,
    But hee clinged to itt with might and maine;
Under the coller then of his iacke,
    Stroke was Sir Andrew thorrow the braine.

'Ffight on, my men,' sayes Sir Andrew Bartton,
    'These English doggs they bite soe lowe;
Ffight on for Scottland and Saint Andrew
    Till you heare my whistle blowe!'

With that they borded this noble shipp,
    Soe did they itt with might and maine;
They ffound eighteen score Scotts alive,
    Besids the rest were maimed and slaine.

My lord Haward tooke a sword in his hand,
    And smote of Sir Andrews head;
The Scotts stood by did weepe and mourne,
    But never a word durst speake or say.

With his head they sayled into England againe,
    With right good will, and fforce and main,
And the day beffore Newyeeres even
    Into Thames mouth they came againe.

Now hath our king Sir Andrews shipp,
    Besett with pearles and precyous stones;
Now hath England two shipps of warr,
    Two shipps of war, before but one.

Then King Henerye shiffted his roome;
    In came the Queene and ladyes bright;
Other arrands they had none
    But to see Sir Andrew Bartton, knight.

But when they see his deadly fface,
    His eyes were hollow in his head;
'I wold give a hundred pound,' sais King Henerye,
    'The man were alive as hee is dead!

AROUJ BARBAROSSA

Lesbos, an island in the *Aegean Sea*, gave birth to this bold and enterprising corsair. His father was a Christian by principle, and by profession a potter. At his twentieth year, a *Turkish* half-galley, armed for the cruise, touched at the island. Thither he repaired; and accosting the *Rais*, or Captain, he expressed his willingness to become a *Mussulman*, and to follow his fortunes. The Captain, seeing him a proper, sprightly and promising youth, readily embraced the offer. For some years he followed the trade of scouring the seas, and soon became much noted and highly esteemed, for his intrepidity. Some *Turkish* merchants of *Constantinople*, being no strangers to his character, having built and armed out a galeot, or light gally, made our adventurer a proffer of its command; which employ, he promptly accepted. When he got to sea, he opened his mind to the chiefs of his equipage, laying before them the vast advantages would infallibly accrue to them all, if they bent their course towards *Barbary*, and from thence rifle all the Christians they met with, at discretion. While in the quest of prey, he met with an adventure attended with a success scarce to be equalled in story. *St. Peter's* chair being filled by *Pope Julius II*, two gallies, belonging to his Holiness, richly laden, from *Genoa*, for *Civita Vecchia*, were within sight of *Elba*, when *Arouj Rais* discovered them, as they came, negligently, rowing along, careless, indolently supine, and in very indifferent order. [Here the disproportion between a galley-royal and a galeot ought not to pass unconsidered.] No sooner had this bold *renegado* got sight of them, but he vigorously made towards the nearest and exhorted his men to prepare for the engagement. The *Turks* utterly condemned the madness of the proposal, and plainly told their Captain, that he reflected not; that, instead of offering to be so rash as to attack an enemy so far above their match, they thought it their business to make off with speed, in order to escape such evident danger. *God forbid*, replied the determined corsair, *that I should ever live to be branded with such infamy!* And then, his eyes glowing with indignation and resentment, he fiercely commanded almost all the oars to be thrown over-board. He was instantly obeyed; and thereby, as he intended, no hopes left to his cautious *Turks* of putting in execution what he termed cowardice. Meanwhile the galley approached, not imagining the galeot to be *Turkish*, (a sight till then unknown in those seas). But being arrived near enough to distinguish the *Turkish* habits, in the utmost hurry and apparent consternation, they began to make ready for an encounter. The *Turks*, pouring in their shot and arrows very smartly, killed some *Christians*, wounded many, and terrified all the rest; so that with small opposition and less damage, they immediately boarded, and forced her to a surrendry.

No sooner were the Christians secured under hatches, but *Arouj Rais* signified to his people, that he must, and would have the other galley, which was leisurely advancing towards them, and seemed to know nothing of the matter. In a brief exhortation, he told them, that nothing was required at their hands, but to resolve she should be their prize, and to put on a determined countenance. He then ordered the new captives to be stripped of their clothes, &c. in which his equipage dressed themselves; and, the better to deceive and surprise, the Christians, made all his soldiers pass into the conquered galley, and take in tow the galeot, that it might seem as if the galley had taken a prize. The stratagem failed not of its desired effect. When close enough, the galley was instantly boarded and carried, with very little bloodshed, or resistance. Many *Moors*, and a few *Turks*, whom they found chained to the oar, were set at liberty, a like number of the robustest Christians supplied their places, and our fortunate adventurer hastened away with his two prizes. *How celebrated the name of* Arouj Rais *was become from that very moment; he being held and accounted, by all the world, as a most valiant and enterprising commander: And by reason his beard was extremely red, or carotty, from thenceforwards he was, generally, called* Barba-rossa, *which, in* Italian, *signifies* Red-Beard. He died fighting, to the very last gasp, like a lion, at about 44 years of age. He was a man excessively bold, resolute, daring, enterprizing.

KHEYR-ED-DIN BARBAROSSA

The corsairs, on account of the disastrous fate of *Arouj Barba-rossa,* unanimously chose *Kheyr-ed-din,* his brother, for their prince. He, either in bravery or any other respect, was not a whit inferior to his gallant predecessor. In A.D. 1519, an affair happened which redounded not a little to his reputation. *Don Hugo de Moncada,* a *Spanish* admiral, with upwards of 30 large ships, 8 royal gallies, and many transports, on board of which were several thousands of veteran troops, entered the *Bay of Algiers.* His Catholic majesty, *Don Carlos* (not yet elected Emperor), sent this armada expressly to drive the *Turks* from that country; which he presumed might easily be effected since the defeat and death of the arch-corsair *Barba-rossa.* At sight of this fleet, the inhabitants began to fly the city, till *Kheyr-ed-din* assured them that with the few *Turks* he had, he would not fail protecting them to the last man. Yet the *Spaniards* did not land at all, being prevented by the sudden storm that arose, and the far greater part of the fleet perished. *Kheyr-ed-din* never failed, once, or oftener in a year, going out on cruise, with his galeots, to the infinite detriment of such Christians as he could surprise, or master, for he was not in league with any except the *French,* who were joined in strict alliance with the *Ottomans.* So another mighty Armada was prepared by *Charles the Emperor,* now for the *Tunis* expedition. *Kheyr-ed-din Basha* drew off his *Turks* with much treasure, got fitted out his galeots, and put to sea. In three days he got under *Minorca:* And as it was universally known, that the *Emperor* was at *Tunis,* making war against the *Turkish* corsairs, there was none who were under the least apprehension of being attacked or molested by the very people, whose utter extirpation the *flower of Europe* had so heartily undertaken, and of whose daily successes such mighty things were rumored, that their ruin seemed inevitable: insomuch, that those islanders, as the galeots approached, took them for no other than a squadron detached from the armada. All this was no more than what the insidious *Kheyr-ed-din* had projected; for the better to beguile and confirm them in their error, he hoisted *Spanish, Italian, &c.* colors, and his corsairs, who came in sight, were dressed *a la Christianesca.* Losing no time, the corsairs made up to the town; which, after a feeble resistance, was entered, entirely sacked, fired and laid desolate. Upwards of 6000 persons were made captives, and much valuable booty was carried off, and *Kheyr-ed-din* departed well satisfied with his adventure. The *Emperor* was much displeased at his escape, being extremely ambitious of having in his power so redoubted and so dangerous an enemy.

He took several important places from the *Venetians;* who, terrified at these severe blows, which shook their state, menacing its ruin, purchased a pacification. Soon he was again seen at the head of 100 gallies, endeavoring to crush the exorbitant, growing power of that active and restless monarch, *Charles V.* Passing by *Caietta,* the governor imprudently fired a single shot at him, which so exasperated the choleric *Captain-Basha,* that tho' he had no such design, he immediately landed 12,000 *Turks,* and battered the town, so much in earnest, that he soon got entrance. Among the captives there taken, was the Governor's daughter, a most beautiful damsel, of 18; with whom he became so enamored, that he married her. Then orders came that *Nice* should be attacked. This dear lover of action instantly weighed, and soon began a fierce and terrible battery against the town, utterly destroying all that delightsome neighborhood.

Returning home, at the end of 1545, he bad farewell to the fluid element, and then became employed in building. He erected a most magnificent mosque, and near it a stately dome, for his own sepulcher, near *Constantinople.* In May 1548, this great man was seized with a violent fever, which carried him off, to the general regret of the whole *Turkish* nation, by whom he was highly beloved. The *Turks* report, as a certain truth that his corpse was found, 4 or 5 times, out of the ground. Nor could they, possibly, make him lie quiet in his grave, till a *Greek* wizard counselled them to bury a black dog together with his body; which done, he lay still and gave them no further trouble. The memory of this famous *renegado* is yet held in such veneration among the *Turks,* particularly the sea-faring people, that no voyage is undertaken from *Constantinople* without their first visiting his tomb, whereat they say a *fedha,* or prayer for success.

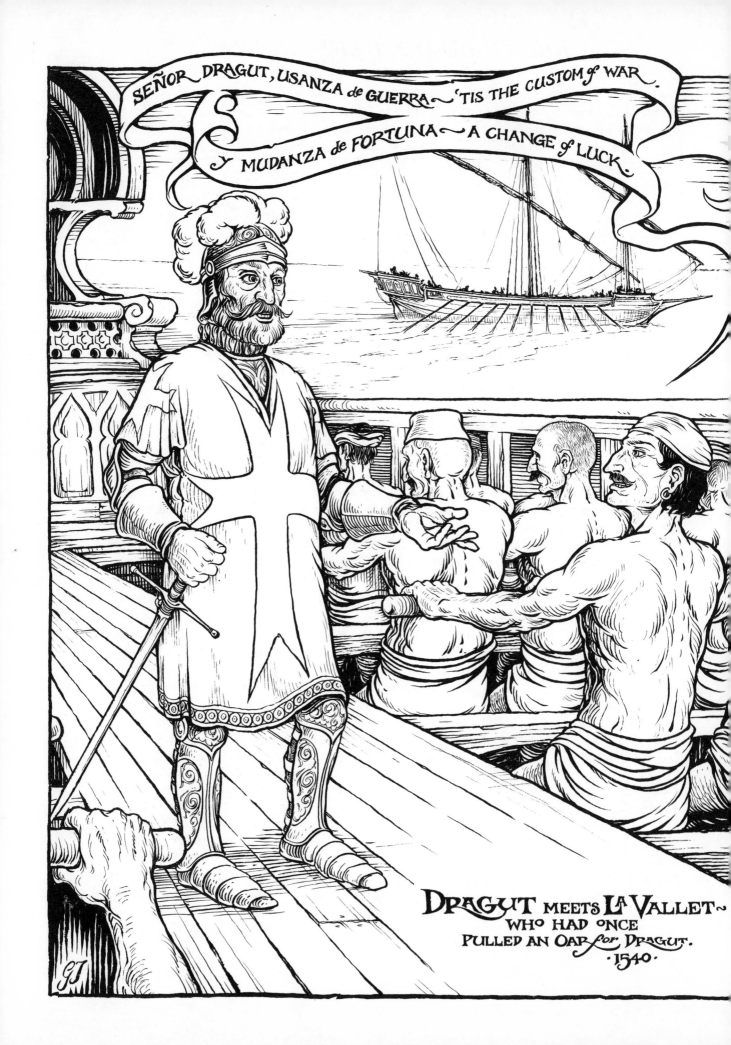

SEÑOR DRAGUT, USANZA de GUERRA ~ 'TIS THE CUSTOM of WAR.
Y MUDANZA de FORTUNA ~ A CHANGE of LUCK.

DRAGUT MEETS LA VALLET ~
WHO HAD ONCE
PULLED AN OAR for DRAGUT.
·1540·

DRAGUT Rais

He was born in *Asia-Minor*, opposite to *Rhodes*; his parents labored in the culture of the land they farmed. This obscure and toilsome life ill agreed with young *Dragut's* sprightly and aspiring genius, so in his twelfth year, he entered into the service of a master-gunner, who served on board the *Grand Signor's* gallies. He rose to be a good pilot and a most excellent gunner, and at last purchased a share in a cruising brigantine: nor was it long before he became sole proprietor of a galeot, with which he took some very considerable prizes. And, increasing in strength, he soon rendered himself formidable throughout the *Levant* parts of the *Mediterranean*. But, as all free-booting *Mussulmans*, frequenting those quarters, must, in some measure, be dependants on *Kheyr-ed-din*, *Dragut Rais* accordingly went to offer him his service at *Algiers*. This corsair's reputation flying before him, *Kheyr-ed-din* was no stranger to his worth, and was overjoyed to entertain so brave and so deserving a mariner.

The Emperor, *Charles V*, ordered his admiral, *Prince Andrea D'Oria*, to hunt him out, and to purge the seas of so insufferable a nuisance. That ancient commander committed this affair to the care of his nephew, who had the good fortune to light on *Dragut* under the coast of *Corsica*. The corsair found himself hemmed in on all hands, and the only method left was to hang out the white flag. Thus, *Dragut* rowed in *Admiral D'Oria's* own galley full four years. But, that term being expired, the *Genoese* were so alarmed to behold the famous *Kheyr-ed-din* enter their river, at the head of 100 gallies, insisting that *Dragut Rais* should be set at liberty, that, to prevent their territory from being ravaged, they instantly sent him on board the *Basha's* galley.

Kheyr-ed-din dying, *Sultan Suliman* commanded all the corsairs of his dominions, to acknowledge *Dragut Rais* for their Captain-General. *Andrea D'Oria* passed the whole summer of 1549 with 43 royal gallies, in a fruitless search of the arch-corsair *Dragut*, who was making terrible havoc everywhere. To his great joy, he soon understood, that *Dragut*, with all his gallies, partly disarmed, lay in the harbor of the island *Jerba*. His unexpected arrival greatly surprised *Dragut*, being thus hemmed in by a superior power, without any visible possibility of escaping. But being a man of a bold, undaunted spirit, he resolved to leave no means unattempted. He set to work to level a way, cross the island, from the place where his fleet lay, to the opposite shore. Athwart this new-made road he laid rafters, covered over with well-tallowed planks. By main strength, all the gallies were, with the utmost silence, hoisted up and placed upon great rollers of wood, and so drawn along one after another in a row; and without abundance of farther difficulty, they again found water, after this unaccountable land-journey. This done, the subtle corsair embarked and hasted away; leaving *Andrea D'Oria* with *the dog to hold*.

In July 1551, the *Ottoman* armada, to the terror of the whole Christian part of the *Mediterranean*, cast anchor under *Malta*. *Fort St. Elmo* was reduced to the last extremity. Its holding out had been wholly owing to the indefatigable vigilance of the brave *De la Valette*, the worthy grand-master, and the insuperably heroic valor of the cavaliers of *Malta*. *Dragut*, this seldom-successless corsair, being advanced to look about and discover the disposition of the ground, was taken on the head by a stone, shattered by a great shot, from *Castle Saint Angelo*, and survived not the reduction of that fort many moments: For some of his officers running to his tent to carry him the news found him just upon his departure. Tho'  he had lost his speech, he seemed eager to know the event: and when they acquainted him with the success, he failed not to express his joy and satisfaction by gestures. When lifting up his eyes towards heaven, as if in thanksgiving for such welcome tidings, he instantly expired.

PIERRE le GRAND

The first pirate that was known upon the island of *Tortuga* was named *Pierre le Grand*, or *Peter the Great*. He was born at the town of *Dieppe*, in *Normandy*. The action which rendered him famous was his taking of the *Vice-Admiral* of the *Spanish* flota, near the *Cape of Tiburon*, upon the western side of the island of *Hispaniola*. This bold exploit he performed alone with only one boat, wherein he had eight and twenty persons, no more, to help him. What gave occasion to this enterprise was that until that time the *Spaniards* had passed and repassed with all security, and without finding the least opposition, through the *Bahama Channel*. So that *Pierre le Grand* set out to sea by the *Caicos*, where he took this great ship with almost all facility imaginable. The *Spaniards* they found aboard were all set on shore, and the vessel presently sent into *France*. The manner how this undaunted spirit attempted and took such an huge ship, I shall give you out of the journal of a true and faithful author, in the same words as I read.

The boat, he says, *wherein* Pierre le Grand *was with his companions, had now been at sea a long time, without finding anything, according to his intent of piracy, suitable to make a prey. And now their provisions beginning to fail, they could keep themselves no longer upon the ocean, or they must of necessity starve. Being almost reduced to despair, they espied a great ship belonging to the* Spanish *flota, which had separated from the rest. This bulky vessel they resolved to set upon and take, or die in the attempt. Hereupon they made sail towards her, with design to view her strength. And although they judged the vessel to be far above their forces, yet the covetousness of such a prey, and the extremity of fortune they were reduced to, made them adventure on such an enterprise. Being now come so near that they could not escape without danger of being all killed, the pirates jointly made an oath to their captain,* Pierre le Grand, *to behave themselves courageously in this attempt, without the least fear or fainting. True it is, that these rovers had conceived an opinion that they should find the ship unprovided to fight, and that through this occasion they should master her by degrees.*

It was in the dusk of the evening, or soon after, when this great action was performed. But before it was begun, they gave orders to the surgeon of the boat to bore a hole in the sides thereof, to the intent that, their own vessel sinking under them, they might be compelled to attack more vigorously, and endeavor more hastily to run aboard the great ship. This was performed accordingly; and without any other arms than a pistol in one of their hands and a sword in the other, they immediately climbed up the sides of the ship, and ran altogether into the great cabin, where they found the Captain, with several of his companions, playing at cards. Here they set a pistol to his breast, commanding him to deliver up the ship to their obedience. The Spaniards *seeing the pirates aboard their ship, without scarce having seen them at sea, cried out,* Jesus bless us! Are these devils, or what are they? *In the meanwhile some of them took possession of the gun-room, and seized the arms and military affairs they found there, killing as many of the ship as made any opposition. By which means the* Spaniards *were presently compelled to surrender. That very day the Captain of the ship had been told by some of the seamen that the boat, which was in view cruising, was a boat of pirates. To whom the Captain, slighting their advice, made answer:* What then? Must I be afraid of such a pitiful thing as that is? No, nor though she were a ship as big and as strong as mine is.

As soon as Pierre le Grand *had taken this magnificent prize, he detained in his service as many of the common seamen as he had need of, and the rest he set on shore. This being done, he immediately set sail for* France, *carrying with him all the riches he found in that huge vessel: here he continued without ever returning to the parts of* America.

BARTOLOMEW PORTUGUES
WHO COMMITTED INNUMERABLE EXCESSIVE INSOLENCES UPON THE COASTS, 1666.

BARTHOLOMEW PORTUGUES

A certain pirate, born in *Portugal,* and from the name of his country called *Bartholomew Portugues,* was cruising in his boat from *Jamaica* to the island of *Cuba.* He met with a great ship, bound for the *Havana,* which he presently assaulted, and after a long and dangerous fight he became master of it.

Having possessed such a ship, he resolved to steer toward the western side of the isle of *Cuba,* being now very near. He unexpectedly met with three great ships that were coming from *New Spain.* By these as not being able to escape, the pirates were all made prisoners, and stripped of all the riches they had pillaged so little before. The great vessel wherein the pirates were, arrived at *Campeche,* where many considerable merchants knew the *Portuguese* pirate, as being him who had committed innumerable excessive insolences upon those coasts.

Fearing least the captain of those pirates should escape, they judged it more convenient to leave him safely guarded on board the ship for the present. In the meanwhile they caused a gibbet to be erected, whereupon to hang him the very next day. The rumor of this future tragedy was presently brought to *Bartholomew Portugues*'ears, whereby he sought all the means he could to escape that night. With this design he took two earthen jars, wherein the *Spaniards* usually carry wine from *Spain* to the *West Indies,* and stopped them very well, intending to use them for swimming. Having made this necessary preparation, he waited for the night, when all should be asleep, even the sentry that guarded him. He then committed himself to sea with those two earthen jars, and by their help and support, though never having learned to swim, he reached the shore.

Those of the city failed not the next day to make a diligent search for him in the woods, where they concluded him to be. This strict enquiry *Portugues* had the convenience to espy from the hollow of a tree, wherein he lay absconded. Hence perceiving them to return without finding what they sought for, he adventured to sally forth towards the coasts, where he made as well as he could a boat, or rather a raft. Thus he happened to find a certain vessel of pirates, who were great comrades of his own. To these he instantly demanded that they would fit him with a boat and 20 men, with which company alone he promised to return to *Campeche* and assault the ship which he had been taken by and escaped from. They readily granted his request, and with this small company he set forth.

Being arrived at *Campeche,* with undaunted courage and without any rumor of noise, he assaulted the ship beforementioned, and in short space of time compelled the *Spaniards* to surrender. Being now masters of the ship, they immediately weighed anchor and set sail. *Portugues,* now by a second turn of Fortune's wheel was become rich and powerful again, who had been so lately in that same vessel a poor miserable prisoner and condemned to the gallows. But coming near the isle of *Pinos,* Fortune turned her back upon him once more, never to show him her countenance again. For a horrible storm arising at sea occasioned the ship to split against the rocks.

FRANCIS L'OLLONAIS

Francis L'Ollonais was a native of *France*. In his youth he was transported to the *Caribee Islands*, in quality of a servant or slave, according to the custom of *France* and other countries. When he had obtained his freedom, he came to the *Isle of Hispaniola*. Here he placed himself for some while among the hunters, before he began his robberies against the *Spaniards*. At first he made 2 or 3 voyages in quality of a common mariner, wherein he behaved himself so courageously as to deserve the favor and esteem of the *Governor* of *Tortuga*; insomuch that this gentleman gave him a ship and made him captain thereof. In a short time he pillaged great riches, but withal, his cruelties against the *Spaniards* were such that the very fame of them made him known through the whole *Indies*. But in a huge storm he lost his ship upon the coasts of *Campeche*. The men were all saved; but coming upon dry land, the *Spaniards* pursued them, and killed the greatest part of them, wounding also *L'Ollonais*, their captain. After the *Spaniards* were gone, he retired into the woods, and bound up his wounds as well as he could. Then he took his way to the city of *Campeche*, disguised in *Spanish* habit. Here he spoke with certain slaves, to whom he promised their liberty, in case they would obey him and trust in his conduct. They accepted his promises, and stealing one night a canoe, they went to sea with the pirate. *L'Ollonais* came safe to *Tortuga*, the common place of refuge of all sorts of wickedness, the seminary, as it were, of all manner of pirates and thieves.

Though now his fortune was but low, yet he failed not of means to get another ship, which with craft and subtlety he obtained. He then set forth towards the *Isle of Cuba*, greatly persuaded he should get here some considerable prey, but the inhabitants complained to the *Governor* that *L'Ollonais* was come to destroy them. At the importunity of the petitioners the *Governor* sent a ship to their relief, well armed, giving them withal this express command: They should not return unto his presence without having totally destroyed the pirates. The pirates were advertised beforehand of the coming of this ship, and, instead of flying, went to seek the said vessel, hoping soon to obtain a greater vessel than their canoes, and thereby to mend their fortune. About the break of day the pirates began to assault the vessel. This attack they performed with such vigor that the *Spaniards* were forced to surrender, after being beaten by the pirates, with swords in hand, down under the hatches. Hence *L'Ollonais* commanded them to be brought up one by one, and in this order caused their heads to be struck off. He sent back to the *Governor* of *Havana*, with this message: *I shall never henceforward give quarter to any Spaniard whatsoever; and I have great hopes I shall execute on your own person the very same punishment I have done upon them you sent against me.*

Now *L'Ollonais* had got himself a good ship; hereupon, he resolved to go to the port of *Maracaibo*, where he took by surprise a ship that was laden with plate and other merchandise. With these prizes he returned to *Tortuga*, where he was received with no small joy. He continued not long there, but pitched upon new designs of equipping a whole fleet, sufficient to transport 500 men. With these preparations he resolved to go to the *Spanish* dominions, and pillage both cities, towns and villages, and finally take *Maracaibo* itself. For this purpose, he knew that the *Island of Tortuga* would afford him many resolute and courageous men. They set sail, and, suddenly espied a ship that was coming from *Porto Rico*, bound for *New Spain*. The *Spaniards* knew them to be pirates, yet they would not flee, but rather prepared to fight. Thus the combat began, which lasted 3 hours; and these being past, they surrendered to him. They found in this ship 120,000 weight of cacao, 40,000 pieces of eight, and the value of 10,000 more in jewels. *L'Ollonais* sent the vessel presently to *Tortuga* to be unloaded. Full of courage, they set sail for *Maracaibo*, which port is situated in the province of *New Venezuela;* the city may possibly have contained 3 or 4,000 persons, which made a town of reasonable bigness. This city having formerly been taken by such kind people as these were, and sacked even to the remotest corners thereof, preserved still within its memory a fresh idea of that misery. Hereupon as soon as they heard the dismal news, they endeavored to escape as fast as they could, carrying with them all the goods and money they could.

The pirates marched in good order into the town, whose inhabitants, were all retired into the woods. Their houses they left well provided with all sort of victuals, and with these things the pirates fell to banqueting and making good cheer. The next day they sent to find out some of the inhabitants of the town; these prisoners were put to the rack, only to make them confess where they had hidden the rest of their goods, but they could extort very little from them.

L'Ollonais who never used to make any great account of murdering, though, in cold blood, 10 or 12 *Spaniards*, drew his cutlass and hacked one to pieces in the presence of all the rest, saying: *If you do not confess and declare where you have hidden the rest of your goods, I will do the likes to all your companions.* The pirates then sent to tell the governor and inhabitants: They should bring them 30,000 pieces of eight on board their ships, for a ransom of their houses; otherwise they should be entire sacked and burnt. The *Spaniards* concluded with the pirates they would give for their ransom and liberty the sum of 20,000 pieces of eight and 500 cows, the condition hereof being that they should depart thence presently after payment. This being delivered, they set sail with the whole fleet, causing great joy to the inhabitants of *Maracaibo*.

The pirates, casting anchor in a port called *Cow Island*, made a dividend amongst them of all their prizes and gains. Having cast up the account and made exact calculation of all they had purchased, they found in ready money 260,000 pieces of eight. They weighed all the plate that was uncoined, reckoning after the rate of 10 pieces of eight for every pound. This being done, everyone was put to his oath again, that he had not concealed anything nor subtracted from the common stock. The whole dividend being entirely finished, they set sail thence for the *Isle of Tortuga*. Here they arrived, to the great joy of most that were upon the island. For as to the common pirates, in 3 weeks they had scarce any money left them; having spent it all in things of little value, or at play either at cards or dice. The taverns, according to the custom of pirates, got the greatest part thereof. *L'Ollonais* had got himself very great esteem and repute at *Tortuga* by this last voyage, by reason he brought them home such considerable profit. And now he needed take no great care how to gather men to serve under his colors. He resolved therefore for a second voyage, to go towards the parts of *Nicaragua*, and pillage there as many towns as he could meet.

He set sail, and took many prisoners, and committed upon them the most insolent and inhuman cruelties that ever heathens invented, putting them to the cruellest tortures he could imagine or devise. It was the custom of *L'Ollonais* that, having tormented any persons and they not confessing, he would instantly cut them to pieces with his hanger, and pull out their tongues, desiring to do the same, if possible, to every *Spaniard* in the world. Some prisoners were asked by *L'Ollonais* if there was no other way to be found to the neighboring town, distant 10 or 12 leagues, than through ambuscades. Finding they could show him no other way, *L'Ollonais* grew outrageously passionate; insomuch that he drew his cutlass, and with it cut open the breast of one of those poor *Spaniards*, and pulling out his heart with his sacrilegious hands, began to bite and gnaw it with his teeth, like a ravenous wolf, saying to the rest: *I will serve you all alike, if you show me not another way.* Hereupon those miserable wretches promised to show him another way.

L'Ollonais having set sail, arrived in a few days at the mouth of the river of *Nicaragua*. Here suddenly his ill-fortune assailed him, which of long time had been reserved for him, as a punishment due to the multitude of horrible crimes, which in his licentious and wicked life he had committed. Here he met with both *Spaniards* and *Indians*, who jointly together set upon him and his companions, and used them so roughly that the greatest part of the pirates were killed upon the place. *L'Ollonais* had much ado to escape. And God Almighty, the time of His Divine Justice being now already come, had appointed the *Indians* to be the instruments and executioners thereof. The *Indians* within a few days after his arrival took him prisoner and tore him in pieces alive, throwing his body limb by limb into the fire and his ashes into the air; to the intent no trace nor memory might remain of such an infamous inhuman creature.

Thus ends the life of that infernal wretch *L'Ollonais*, who, full of horrid, execrable deeds, and debtor to so much innocent blood, died by cruel and butcherly hands.

There have been some other pirates, besides those whose history is here related, and their adventures are as extravagant and full of mischief, as those who are the subject of this book. Here is a flag of some wicked pirates of Barbary, from where, for centuries, was pestered the shipping of the Mediterranean Sea until stopped by the glorious United States Navy and the heroic Marines.

A FLAG of the BARBARY PIRATES · 1707

Ensign at Mizen Peak
of Capt. BARTH.º ROBERTS

JACK of
Capt. BARTH.º ROBERTS

JOLLY ROGER, flag of
Capt.ˢ ROBERTS, LOW, SPRIGGS, &ᶜ.

Long BEN AVERY

Major BONNET

Calico JACK RACKAM

Capt. ENGLAND

Pennant · 1704

Capt. WYNNE

Capt. TEW

French · FILIBUSTER

"A BLACK FLAG," THEY MERRILY SAID, "WOULD BE AS GOOD AS FIFTY MEN."

Captain AVERY

None of these bold adventurers were ever so much talked of as *Avery*. He made a great noise in the world, and was represented as one that had raised himself to the dignity of a king, having, as it was said, taken immense riches, and married the *Great Mogul's* daughter, and was living in great royalty and state. A play was writ upon him, called, the *Successful Pirate*, and some were for inviting him to *England*, with all his treasure, least he hinder the trade of *Europe*. He was born in the west of *England* near *Plymouth*. Being bred to the sea, he served as a mate of a merchant-man, in several trading voyages. It happened that the *French* in *Martinico*, carry'd on a smuggling trade with the *Spaniards* on the continent of *Peru*, which by the laws of *Spain*, is not allowed. Now, the *Spaniards* being poorly provided with ships, it was resolved in *Spain*, to hire two or three stout foreign ships for their service. Some merchants of *Bristol* fitted out two ships; the hire being agreed for, they were commanded to sail for *Spain*. Of one of these ships, *Avery* was first mate, and being a fellow of more cunning, than courage, he insinuated himself into the good will of several of the boldest fellows on board, finding them ripe to run away with the ship, telling them what great wealth was to be had upon the coast of *India*. When our gentry saw that all was clear, they secured the hatches and put to sea. The *Captain*, who by this time, was awaked, rung the bell. *Avery* went into the cabin; the *Captain*, half asleep, ask'd, *What was the matter? Come,* says *Avery, and I'll let you into a secret:—I am* Captain *of this ship now, and this is my cabin, therefore you must walk out; I am bound to* Madagascar, *with a design of making my own fortune, and that of all the brave fellows joined with me.*

They proceeded on their voyage to *Madagascar*, and then steered towards the *Arabian* coast. Near the river *Indus*, the man at the mast-head spied a sail, upon which they gave chase, and as they came nearer to her, they perceiv'd her to be a tall ship, and fancy'd she might be a *Dutch East-India* man homeward bound; but she proved a better prize. When they fired at her to bring to, she hoisted *Mogul's* colors, soon struck and yielded. She was one of the *Great Mogul's* own ships, and there were in her several of the greatest persons of his court, among whom it was said was one of his daughters, who were going on a pilgrimage to *Mecca*, the *Mahometans* thinking themselves obliged once in their lives to visit that place; and they were carrying with them rich offerings to present at the shrine of *Mahomet*. It is known that the eastern people travel with the utmost magnificence, so that they had with them all their slaves and attendants, their rich habits and jewels, and vessels of gold and silver, and great sums of money to defray the charges of their journey by land; wherefore the plunder got by this prize, is not easily computed. As soon as the news came to the *Mogul*, and he knew that they were *English* who had robbed them, he threatened loud, and talked of sending a mighty army with fire and sword, to extirpate the *English* from all their settlements on the *Indian* coast. The *East-India Company* were very much alarmed at it; however, by degrees, they found means to pacify him, by promising to do their endeavors to take the robbers, and deliver them into his hands; however, the great noise this thing made in *Europe* was the occasion of all the romantic stories formed of *Avery's* greatness. *Avery*, and his men, having then consulted what to do with themselves, came to a resolution, to make the best of their way towards *America*; and none of them being known in those parts, they intended to divide the treasure, to change their names, to go ashore, and live at ease. At length he came to *Boston*, in *New-England*, and seem'd to have a desire of settling in those parts, but he changed his resolution, and proposed to sail for *Ireland*. He found out that *New-England* was not a proper place for him, because a great deal of his wealth lay in diamonds; and should he have produced them there, he would have certainly been seized on suspicion of piracy. But in *Dublin*, he was afraid to offer his diamonds to sale, least an enquiry into his manner of coming by them should occasion a discovery. Therefore he consulted with friends about the means of his effects. They agreed that the safest method would be, to put them in the hands of some merchants, who gave him a little money for his present subsistance. In some time his little money was spent, yet he heard nothing from his merchants. He writ to them often, and after much importunity they sent him but scarce sufficient to pay his debts, wherefore, being weary of his life, he went privately to speak to the merchants himself, where, instead of money, he met a most shocking repulse. For when he desired them to come to an account with him, they silenced him, by threatening to discover him, so that our merchants were as good pirates at land as he was at sea. *Avery* was soon reduced to beggary; in this extremity he was but a few days, before he fell sick and died; not being worth as much as would buy him a coffin.

Captain WILLIAM KIDD

We now give an account of one whose name is better known than most whose histories we have already related. The person is *Captain Kidd*, whose trial and execution have been chanted about in ballads. In *King William's War*, *Captain Kidd* commanded a privateer and acquired the reputation of a brave man and experienced seaman. About this time the pirates were very troublesome in these parts, wherefore *Captain Kidd* was recommended by the *Lord Bellamont* as a person very fit for cruising upon pirates, being acquainted with all their lurking places.

He sail'd out of *Plymouth* in May 1696, in the *Adventure Galley* of 30 guns, and 80 men. The place he first design'd for was *New-York*. When he arrived there, he encreas'd his company to 155 men, and sail'd to *Madagascar*, the rendezvous of pirates, where he arrived in 1697. It happened that the pirate ships were most of them out in search of prey, so there was not one of them about, wherefore he thought of trying his fortune on the *Coast of Malabar*. Hereabouts he made an unsuccessful cruise. His provisions were wasting, but it does not appear that he had the least design of turning pirate; for he met with several *Indian* ships richly loaden, to which he did not offer violence. The first outrage or depredation I find he committed upon Mankind, was upon the *Red Sea*, where he took some *Guiney* corn from the natives.

CAPT KIDD IS SEDUCED by THE INSTIGATIONS of THE DEVIL.

Here he began to open himself to his ship's company, and let them understand that he intended to change his measures. For, happening to talk of the *Mocha Fleet* which was to sail that way, he said, *We have been unsuccessful hitherto, but courage, my boys, we'll make our fortunes out of this fleet.* And finding that none of them appear'd averse to it, he order'd a boat to go upon the coast to make discoveries. The boat return'd, bringing him word that they saw 14 or 15 ships ready to sail. We cannot account for this sudden change in his conduct, otherwise than by supposing that he first meant well, while he had hopes of making his fortune by taking of pirates. But weary of ill success, and fearing least his owners, out of humor, at their great expences, should dismiss him, and he should want employment, and, rather than run the hazard of poverty, he resolved to do his business one way, since he could not do it another.

The first prize he met was a small vessel belonging to *Moorish* merchants. He seem'd to have some fears upon him lest these proceedings should have a bad end, for, coming up with a *Dutch* ship when his men thought of attacking her, *Kidd* oppos'd it; upon which a mutiny arose. And *Moore*, the gunner, talking with *Kidd* about the said *Dutch* ship, some words arose betwixt them, and *Moore* told *Kidd*, that he had ruin'd them all. Upon which, *Kidd*, calling him dog, took up a bucket and struck him with it, which breaking his skull, he died the next day.

The greatest prize which fell into his hands, while he followed this trade, was a *Moorish* ship of 400 tons richly loaden, named the *Queda Merchant*. *Kidd* gave the owners to understand, that if they would offer anything worth taking for their ransom, he would hearken to it. Upon which they proposed 20,000 rupees, but *Kidd* rejected it, and he soon sold as much of the cargo as came to near 10,000 pounds.

Kidd put some of his men on board the *Queda Merchant*, and sail'd for *Madagascar*. As soon as he was arrived, there came on board a canoe, in which were several *Englishmen*. As soon as they saw him they saluted him, and told him, they were informed he was come to take them, and hang them, which would be a little unkind in such an old acquaintance. *Kidd* dissipated their doubts, swearing he was now their brother, and as bad as they. The *Adventure Galley* was now leaky, wherefore *Kidd* shifted all the guns into the *Queda Merchant*. He happened to touch at *Amboyna*, where he was told, that the news of his actions had reach'd *England*, and he was there declared a pirate. But relying upon *Lord Bellamont*, and fancying, that a *French* pass or two he found on board some of the ships he took, would serve to countenance the matter — I say, all these things made him flatter himself that all would be hushed, and that Justice would but wink at him. —Wherefore he sail'd directly for *New-York*, where he was no sooner arrived, but by the *Lord Bellamont's* orders, he was secured. A Session of Admiralty being held at the *Old Baily*, in 1701, *Captain Kidd* and his fellow-adventurers, were arraign'd for piracy on the High Seas, and found guilty. *Kidd* was try'd upon an indictment of murder also for killing *Moore* the gunner, and found guilty of the same.

As to *Kidd's* defense, he insisted much upon his own innocence, and the villainy of his men. He said, he went out in a laudable employment, and had no occasion to go a-pirating; that the men being a parcel of rogues and villains, mutinied against him, and did as they pleased; that he was threatened to be shot in his cabin, that the prizes he took were taken by virtue of a commission, they having *French* passes. The Captain called one to his reputation, who gave him an extraordinary character, and declared to the court, that he had served under his command, and been in two engagements with him against the *French*, in which he fought as well as any man he ever saw; but this being several years before the facts mentioned in the indictment were committed, prov'd of no manner of service to the prisoner on his trial. The evidence being full and particular against him, he was found guilty; when asked what he had to say why sentence should not pass against him, he answered, that he had nothing to say, but that he had been sworn against by perjured, wicked people. And when sentence was pronounced, he said, *My Lord, it is a very hard sentence. For my part, I am the innocentest person of them all.* Wherefore about a week after, *Captain Kidd* was executed and afterwards hung up in chains, and his body hung exposed for many years.

Captain MISSON & LIBERTALIA.

Captain Misson, with a crew of brave fellows, resolved upon a *life of liberty*. The boatswain then asked what colors they should fight under, and advised black as most terrifying; but the lieutenant objected: *Ours is a brave, a just, an innocent, and a noble cause; the* cause of liberty. *I advise a white ensign, with liberty painted in the fly, and if you like the motto*, A Deo a Libertate, For God and Liberty, *as an emblem of our uprightness and resolution.* The men, who lent an attentive ear, cry'd, *Liberty, Liberty; we are freemen.*

The captain was satisfy'd men who were born and bred in slavery, by which their spirits were broke, who, ignorant of their birth-right, and the sweets of liberty, dance to the music of their chains, which was, indeed, the greater part of the inhabitants of the globe, would brand this generous crew with the invidious name of *pirates* and think it meritorious, to be instrumental in their destruction.—Self-preservation therefore, and not a cruel disposition, obliged him to declare war against all such as should not immediately surrender and give up what their necessities required. They took a sloop, bound for *Boston*, and then consulted upon the course they should steer. Some were for the *New-England* coast; and that as they were not far from the *English* settlement of *Carolina*, they might either on that or the coast of *Virginia, Maryland, Pennsylvania, New-York,* or *New-England*, intercept ships which traded to the islands with provisions. But the captain was for going to the coast of *Guiney*, where the *East-India* ships drained *Europe* of what money they drew from *America*. On their arrival on the *Gold-Coast*, they fell in with a ship that had but begun to trade for slaves. The *Captain* told his men, that the trading for those of our own species, cou'd never be agreeable to the eyes of divine justice: that no man had power of the liberty of another; that he had not exempted his neck from the galling yoke of *slavery*, and asserted his own liberty, to enslave others, for he abhorr'd even the name of *slavery*. They stretched over to *Madagascar*, and enter'd a bay, where, on account of the wholesomeness of the air, the captain determined to raise a town, that they might have some place to call their own. This settlement was *Libertalia*.

Captain QUELCH

The offenses for which *Quelch* was tried were committed on board the *Charles*, owned by merchants of *Boston*, which was fitted out as a privateer against the *French*. Prior to her sailing, the crew locked the commander into the cabin, and then, under the command of *Quelch*, made for the *South Atlantic*. Some time after, the captain was thrown overboard, but whether alive or dead it does not appear. Off the coast of *Brazil*, it appears that they captured nine vessels, all the property of subjects of the *King of Portugal*, an ally of the *Queen of England*, and from them they took various commodities including 100 weight of gold-dust, gold and silver coins to the value of 1000 pounds or more, etc. No tidings of the *Charles* appear until May, 1704, when her arrival was announced in the *Boston News-Letter*. They had not been long on shore before so many circumstances transpired leading to the suspicion that they had committed acts of piracy against subjects of the *King of Portugal*, and that the story which they had invented of recovering great treasure from a wreck began to be doubted. *Judge Sewall* tells what followed:

Wednesday, June 7th, 1704, *we receiv'd an order from the Governor to search for and seize pirates and their treasure at* Marblehead, *because* Capt. Quelch *in the* Charles *galley arrived there. But matters went heavily, 'twas difficult to get men. The wickedness and despair of the company pursued, their great guns and other warlike preparations, were a terror to most of the town.* June 12th, *good success at the* Isles Sholes, *where three of the pirates were, and so quickly finish'd this business thoroughly without striking a stroke, or firing a gun.* June 30, 1704, *after dinner, about 3 p.m. I went to see the execution. But when I came to see how the river was cover'd with people, I was amazed: Some say there were 100 boats.* Mr. Cotton Mather *came with* Captain Quelch *and six others for execution from the prison to* Scarlet's Wharf, *and from thence in the boat to the place of execution. When the scaffold was let to sink, there was such a screech of the women that my wife heard it sitting next the orchard, and was much surprised at it; yet the wind was sou-west. Our house is a full mile from the place.*

THOU WOULDNST NOT SUFFER THEM TO CONTINUE IN THE GALL OF BITTERNESS & THE BOND OF INIQUITY, & IN THE POSSESSION OF THE DEVIL!!

OLDE NICK

REV. COTTON MATHER of the NORTH CHURCH, BOSTON.

A grab & a galleywat

ANGRIA the PIRATE

In the year 1715, I arrived at *Bombay* with the *Governor* of all the United Company's forces, on the coast of *India, Persia,* and *Arabia.* When the *Governor* arrived, the inhabitants complained of the heavy oppressions and injuries they had received from *Angria* the pirate, whose harbor is very difficult to find out. We had an account of several insults he had offered in those parts on the company's shipping. But I think it proper first to give an account of *Angria.*

At the marriage of *King Charles the Second* with *Catherine of Portugal,* the island of *Bombay* with the cities of *Goa* and *Bassean* were given to *England* as part of her portion. But the *English* met with many interruptions before they obtained it, and the government was obliged to fit out four men of war to settle things for the East-India Company. The *Portuguese* at the resigning *Bombay* to the *English,* quitted the island of *Kenerey* also, which *Angria* made himself master of, and attacked the fishermen of *Bombay* and took some of them. This trifling insult the *English* put up for the present. *Angria* soon increased his number of people and he had several small galleywats with guns. In cruising off the island, they took a large grab belonging to the *Portuguese*; *Angria* mounted several guns on her, and declared open war with all nations, and soon after took another grab of considerable force from the *Portuguese.*

I shall now speak of his first assault on the *English. Capt. Cooke,* chief engineer for the company's fortifications at *Bengal,* his lady and two daughters, came to *Carwar,* on the coast of *India,* then under the protection of *Thomas Harvey, Esq., Governor* of that factory, who entertained them in a splendid manner. *Governor Harvey* took a very great liking to *Capt. Cooke's* eldest daughter, *Mrs. Catherine Cook* on whom he proferr'd to make great settlements, provided the father and mother would consent to her marriage with him, which they did, tho' a very disagreeable match; for *Governor Harvey* was a deform'd man, and in years; she a most beautiful lady, not exceeding thirteen or fourteen years of age, who to oblige her parents consented also. In a short time after they were married. In less than a year after he died, and left his lady chief executrix of all his possessions. She soon after married *Mr. Chown,* a gentleman more suitable to her years than the former; and *Mr. Chown* and she being obliged to come up to *Bombay,* and after all their business was completed there, he was appointed *Governor* of the factory at *Carwar.* This lady being then big with child, the *Governor* of *Bombay* ordered the company's yacht and a small man of war to convoy them to *Carwar*: They set sail but had not lost sight of *Bombay* before *Angria* attack'd them with his grabs, and they begun a smart and bloody battle. The new-made *Governor* had his right arm shot off, and bled to death in the young lady's arms, for want of the assistance of a surgeon. He desired before he expired, if she should alter her condition, to accept of *Mr. William Gifford,* one of the *Council* of the *Island of Bombay*; which she promised.

In a short time they were overcome by the *Angrians,* and carried prisoners into *Kenerey.* The *Defiance,* the small frigate, got safe back to *Bombay,* and gave an account of this to the *President* and *Council*; who directly treated for her ransom, which was 30,000 *rupees.* This the gentlemen of the island soon disburs'd, and made a peace with *Angria,* which he kept for about two years after. The gentlemen who were sent to pay the ransom were obliged to wrap their clothes about her, to cover her nakedness. At her return to *Bombay,* she was welcomed by the chief gentlemen and ladies of the island, who also condol'd her on the loss of so tender a husband. She was shortly after brought to bed of a son. She endured *Angria's* insults beyond expectation. A very short time after her delivery, she was, with the *President's* approbation, married to *Mr. William Gifford,* with whom she lived happily, till he was sent down to *Anjango,* as *Governor* of the company's forts and factory, where he was cut off by the natives.

Captain BELLAMY

As we cannot, with any certainty, deduce this man from his origin, we shall begin where we find him first, a declared enemy to mankind. *Captain Bellamy* had been upon a *Spanish* wreck, and not finding his expectation answered, decided to go upon the account, a term among pirates, which speaks their profession. The first who had the misfortune to fall in his way, was a galley whose cargo consisted of elephants' teeth, gold-dust, and other rich merchandise. He immediately mounted this galley with 28 guns, and put aboard 150 hands. *Bellamy* was declared *Captain*, and the vessel had her old name continued, which was *Whidaw*. They shaped their course for *Virginia*, which coast they very much infested, taking several vessels. They were upon lifting this station, when they were very near, as the psalmist expresses it, *going quick down into Hell*, for the Heavens beginning to lower, prognosticated a storm. *Bellamy* took in all his small sails, and double reefed his main-sail, which was hardly done when a thunder shower overtook them with such violence, that the *Whidaw* was very near oversetting. The storm encreased towards night, and all they could do was to keep her head to the sea. The heavens were cover'd with sheets of lightning, which the sea by the agitation of the saline particles seem'd to imitate; the darkness of the night was such, as the Scripture says, as might be felt. The terrible hollow roaring of the winds, could be only equalled by the repeated, I may say, incessant claps of thunder, sufficient to strike a dread of the Supreme Being, who commands the sea and the winds, one would imagine in every heart. But among these wretches, the effect was different, for they endeavored by their blasphemies, oaths, and horrid imprecations, to drown the uproar of jarring elements. *Bellamy* swore he was sorry he could not run out his guns to return the salute, meaning the thunder, that he fancy'd the Gods had got drunk over their tipple, and were gone together by the ears.

The next morning the main-mast being sprung in the step, they were forced to cut it away, and, at the same time, the mizen came by the board. These misfortunes made the ship ring with blasphemy, which was encreased, when, by trying the pumps, they found the ship made a great deal of water, tho' by continually plying them, it kept it from gaining upon them. The wind shifting round the compass, made so outrageous and short a sea, that they had little hopes of safety; it broke upon the poop, and wash'd the two men away from the wheel. The wind after four days and three nights abated of its fury, and the weather clearing up, so that they resolv'd for the coast of *Carolina*. They continued this course but a day and a night, when the wind coming about to the southward, they changed their resolution to that of going to *Rhode Island*. All this while the *Whidaw's* leak continued, and it was as much as the lee-pump could do to keep the water from gaining, tho' it was kept continually going. Jury-masts were set up and the crew became very jovial again, and off *Rhode Island*, they took a sloop commanded by *Captain Beer*, belonging to *Boston*, in the latitude of *South-Carolina*, and sunk her, and put the captain ashore. I can't pass by in silence, *Captain Bellamy's* speech to *Captain Beer*. *Damn my blood*, says he; *damn the sloop; damn ye, you are a sneaking puppy, and so are all those who will submit to be governed by laws which rich men have made for their own security, for the cowardly whelps have not the courage otherwise to defend what they get by their knavery; but damn ye altogether: Damn them for a pack of crafty rascals, and you, who serve them, for a parcel of hen-eared numbskulls. They villify us, the scoundrels do, when there is only this difference, they rob the poor under the cover of law, forsooth, and we plunder the rich under the protection of our own courage; had you not better make one of us, than sneak after the asses of those villains for employment?* Captain Beer told him, that his conscience would not allow him to break thro' the laws of God and man. *You are a devlish conscience rascal, damn ye*, reply'd Bellamy, *I am a free prince, and I have as much authority to make war on the whole world, as he who has 100 sail of ships at sea, and an army of 100,000 men in the field; and this my conscience tells me; but there is no arguing with such sniveling puppies who allow superiors to kick them about deck at pleasure.* The *Whidaw's* damage being repaired they pass'd their time very jovially, having taken a vessel off *Cape Cod*, loaden with wine. They thought of cruising again and steer'd for *Newfoundland*; there they made some prizes on the banks, and then resolved to visit again the coast of *New-England*. They ran down this coast, and near *Nantucket's* shoals, took the *Mary Anne*, but the master, seeing all the pirates drunk, laid hold on the opportunity, and run his vessel and the *Whidaw* ashore about midnight, near *Eastham*, out of which 7 alone escap'd with life. The pirates were seiz'd by the inhabitants, and imprison'd, condemn'd, and executed at *Boston*.

Captain TEACH alias BLACK-BEARD

Edward Teach was a *Bristol* man born, but had sailed some time out of *Jamaica*, in privateers. Yet tho' he had often distinguished himself for his uncommon boldness and personal courage, he was never raised to any command, till he went a-pirating at the latter end of the year 1716.

In 1717, *Teach* sailed for the main of *America*, and got plunder to a considerable value. After cleaning on the coast of *Virginia*, he returned to the *West-Indies*, and made prize of a large *French Guiney*-man and named her the *Queen Ann's Revenge*. They found a ship of *Boston*, called the *Protestant Caesar*. *Teach* hoisted his black colors, and fired a gun. The ship they burnt, after they had plundered her, because some men had been hanged at *Boston* for piracy. They then sailed to *Carolina*, and lay off of *Charles-Town* and took here several ships as they were coming out, all which struck a great terror to the whole province of *Carolina*, that they abandoned themselves to despair, so that the trade of this place was totally interrupted. *Teach* being in want of medicines, resolved to demand a chest from the government of the province. Tho' 'twas the greatest affront that could have been put upon them, they comply'd with the necessity, and sent aboard a chest, valued at between three and four hundred pounds sterling.

From *Charles-Town*, they sailed to *North-Carolina*. *Teach* cultivated a very good understanding with *Charles Eden, Esq*, the Governor. Before he sailed upon his adventures, he married a young creature of about 16 years of age, the Governor performing the ceremony; and this, I have been informed, made *Teach's* 14th wife, whereof, about a dozen might still be living.

In 1718 he steered towards *Bermuda* and met with 2 or 3 *English* vessels in his way, and 2 *French* ships, one of them was loaden with sugar and cocoa which he brought home with her cargo to *North-Carolina*, where the Governor and the pirates shared the plunder. *Teach* sailed from one inlet to another, trading with such sloops as he met, and took what he liked, without saying by your leave, knowing well they dared not send him a bill for the payment. He often diverted himself with going ashore among the planters, where he revell'd night and day; and often he and his companions took liberties with the wives and daughters of the planters. The sloops pillaged by *Black-beard* consulted with the traders, and some of the best of the planters, what course to take. They sent a deputation to *Virginia*, to lay the affair before the Governor of that colony, and to solicit an armed force from the men of war lying there, to take or destroy this pirate. It was agreed that the Governor should hire a couple of small sloops, and the command of them be given to *Mr. Robert Maynard*, an experienced officer, and a gentleman of great bravery and resolution. The 17th of November, 1718, the Lieutenant sailed from *Hampton*, in *James River* in *Virginia*, and, the 31st in the evening, came to the mouth of *Ocracoke Inlet*, where he got sight of the pirate. *Black-beard* had information of the design and when he had prepared for battle, he set down and spent the night in drinking. One of his men asked him, in case anything should happen to him in the engagement with the sloops, whether his wife knew where he had buried his money? He answered, that nobody but himself, and the *Devil* knew where it was, and the longest liver should take all.

Lieutenant Maynard came to an anchor; for the place being shoal, and the Channel intricate, there was no getting in, where *Teach* lay, that night. But in the morning he weighed, and, coming within gun-shot of the pirate, received his fire; whereupon *Maynard* hoisted the King's colors, and stood directly towards him, with the best way that his sails and oars could make. *Black-beard* cut his cable, and endeavored to make a running fight, keeping a continual fire at his enemies, with his guns. *Mr. Maynard* not having guns, kept a constant fire with small arms, while some of his men labored at their oars. In a little time *Teach's* sloop ran a-ground, and *Mr. Maynard's* drawing more water than that of the pirate, he could not come near him. The Lieutenant ordered all his ballast to be thrown over-board, and all the water to be staved, and then weigh'd and stood for him; upon which *Black-beard* hail'd him in this rude manner: *Damn you for villains, who are you?* The Lieutenant made him answer, *You may see by our colors we are no pirates.* Upon this, *Black-beard* took a glass of liquor, and drank to him with these words: *Damnation seize my soul if I give you quarters, or take any from you.* In answer to which *Mr. Maynard* told him, he expected no quarters from him, nor should he give him any. By this time *Black-beard's* sloop floated, as *Mr. Maynard's* sloops were rowing towards him. The pirate fired a broadside. The sloop the Lieutenant was in, having 20 men killed and wounded, and the other sloop 9: this could not be help'd, for there being no wind, they were obliged to keep to their oars, otherwise the pirate would have got away from him, which, it seems, the Lieutenant was resolute to prevent. After this unlucky blow, he ordered all his men down, for fear of another broadside, which must have been their destruction, and the loss of their expedition. *Mr. Maynard* was the only person that kept the deck, except the man at the helm, whom he directed to lie down snug; and the men in the hold were ordered to get their pistols and their swords ready for close fighting, and to come up at his command. When the Lieutenant's sloop boarded the other, *Captain Teach's* men threw in several new fashion'd sort of grenadoes, but by good Providence, that had no effect here; the men being in the hold. *Black-beard* seeing few or no hands aboard, told his men, that they were all knock'd on the head, except 3 or 4; and therefore, says he, let's jump on board, and cut them to pieces. Whereupon, under the smoke of one of the grenadoes just mentioned, *Black-beard* enters with 14 men, over the bows of *Maynard's* sloop, and were not seen by him till the air cleared; however, he just then gave a signal to his men, who all rose in an instant, and attack'd the pirates with as much bravery as ever was done upon such an occasion: *Black-beard* and the Lieutenant fired the first shots at each other, by which the pirate received a wound, and then engaged with swords, till the Lieutenant's unluckily broke. And stepping back to cock a pistol, *Black-beard*, with his cutlass, was striking at that instant, that one of *Maynard's* men gave him a terrible wound in the neck and throat, by which the Lieutenant came off with only a small cut over his fingers. They were now closely and warmly engaged, the Lieutenant and 12 men against *Black-beard* and 14, till the sea was tinctur'd with blood round the vessel. *Black-beard* received a shot into his body from the pistol that *Lieutenant Maynard* discharg'd, yet he stood his ground, and fought with great fury, till he received 5 and 20 wounds. At length, as he was cocking another pistol, having fired several before, he fell down dead; by which time 8 more out of the 14 dropp'd, and all the rest, much wounded, jump'd over-board and call'd out for quarters, which was granted, tho' it was only prolonging their lives a few days.

Here was an end of that courageous brute, who might have pass'd in the world for a hero, had he been employ'd in a good cause. What seems a little odd, is, that some of these men, who behaved so bravely against *Black-beard*, went afterwards a-pirating themselves, and one of them was taken along with *Roberts*. The Lieutenant caused *Black-beard's* head to be severed from his body, and hung up at the bolt-sprit end. Those of his crew who were taken alive, told a story which may appear a little incredible; however, we think it will not be fair to omit it, since we had it from their own mouths. That once upon a cruise, they found out, that they had a man on board more than their crew; such a one was seen several days amongst them, sometimes below, and sometimes upon deck, yet no man in the ship could give an account who he was or from whence he came; but that he disappeared a little before they were cast away in their great ship, but, it seems, they verily believed it was the *Devil*.

Major STEDE-BONNET

The *Major* was a gentleman of good reputation in the island of *Barbadoes*, and a master of a plentiful fortune. He had the least temptation of any man to follow such a course of life, and was ill qualify'd for the business, as not understanding maritime affairs. However, he fitted out a sloop (the *Revenge*) with ten guns and 70 men, entirely at his own expense, and in the night-time sailed for the capes of *Virginia*, where he took several ships. From hence he went to *New-York*, and off the east end of *Long-Island*, took a sloop. Some time after, *Bonnet* came off of *South-Carolina*, and took a sloop and a brigantine bound in; the brigantine came from *New-England*.

At length he happened to fall in company with another pirate, one *Edward Teach* (who for his remarkably black ugly beard, was more commonly called *Black-beard*): this fellow was a good sailor, but a most cruel hardened villain, bold and daring to the last degree, and would not stick at perpetrating the most abominable wickedness imaginable, for which he was made chief of that execrable gang, *Black-beard* being truly the superior in roguery, as has been already related. To him *Bonnet's* crew joined in consortship, and *Bonnet* himself was laid aside, notwithstanding the sloop was his own. The *Major* now saw his folly, but could not help himself, which made him melancholy; he reflected upon his past course of life, and was confounded with shame, when he thought upon what he had done. His behavior was taken notice of by the other pirates, who liked him never the better for it.

War was now broke out, so *Major Bonnet* gets a clearance for his sloop at *North-Carolina* to go a-privateering upon the *Spaniards*. As the sloop was preparing to sail, a boat informed him that *Captain Teach* lay at *Ocracoke Inlet*, with only 18 or 20 hands. *Bonnet*, who bore him a mortal hatred for some insults, went immediately in pursuit of *Black-beard*, but he missed of him there, and hearing no farther news of him, steered towards *Virginia*.

They chased a sloop of sixty tons, and were so happy as to get a supply of liquor to their victuals. After this, the *Major* threw off all restraint by taking and plundering all the vessels he met with. From *Virginia* they sailed to *Philadelphia*, and took a schooner, coming from *North-Carolina*, bound to *Boston*. Off of *Delaware River*, near *Philadelphia*, they took two ships. At the same time they took a sloop of sixty tons, bound from *Philadelphia*, and a sloop off *Delaware Bay*, bound from *Philadelphia*. Our rovers left *Delaware Bay*, and sailed to *Cape Fear River* where they stayed too long for their safety, for the pirate sloop proved very leaky, so that they were obliged to refit and repair their vessel.

The news came to *Carolina* of a pirate sloop's being there, and the council of *South-Carolina* was alarmed. *Colonel William Rhet* generously offered himself to go with two sloops to attack this pirate. On the 26th of August, 1718, the *Colonel* found *Major Bonnet* and his prizes. The pirates soon discovered the sloops, and they manned three canoes, and sent them down to take them. But they quickly found their mistake, and returned with unwelcome news. *Major Bonnet* made preparations that night for engaging and wrote a letter to the *Governor of Carolina*, that if the sloops were sent out against him, that he would burn and destroy all ships or vessels going in or coming out of *South-Carolina*. The next morning they got under sail; *Colonel Rhet's* sloops got likewise under sail, and stood for *Bonnet*. The pirates beckon'd several times with their hats in derision to the *Colonel's* men, to come on board, and said that they would speak with them by and by; which accordingly happened, for the colonel's sloop being first a-float, the pirates surrender'd themselves prisoners. The *Colonel* took possession of the sloop, and was extremely pleased to find the individual person of *Major Stede Bonnet*, who had done the honor several times to visit their own coast of *Carolina*.

The prisoners made little or no defense, every one pretending only that they were taken off a maroon shore, but being out at sea, and wanting provisions, they were obliged to do what they did by others. And so did *Major Bonnet* himself pretend that 'twas force, not inclination, that occasion'd what had happened. However, the facts being plainly proved, and that they had all shared ten or eleven pounds a man, they were found guilty. The Judge made a very grave speech to them, and then recommended them to the Ministers of the Province for more ample directions, to fit them for eternity. And then pronounced sentence of death upon them. *You, the said* Stede Bonnet, *shall go from hence to the place from whence you came, and from thence to the place of execution, where you shall be hanged by the neck till you are dead.*

Captain HOWEL DAVIS

Captain Howel Davis was born at *Milford, Wales,* and was from a boy brought up to the sea. The last voyage he made from *England* was in the *Cadogan* of *Bristol, Captain Skinner* commander, bound for the coast of *Guiney,* of which snow *Davis* was chief mate: They were no sooner arrived at *Sierraleon* on the aforesaid coast, but they were taken by the pirate *England,* who plunder'd them, and *Skinner* was barbarously murdered. After the death of *Captain Skinner, Davis* pretended that he was mightily solicited by *England* to engage with him; but that he resolutely answered, he would sooner be shot to death than sign the pirates' articles. Upon which *England,* pleased with his bravery, sent him and the rest of the men again on board the *Cadogan,* appointing him captain of her, in the room of *Skinner,* commanding him to pursue his voyage. He also gave him a written paper sealed up, with orders to open it when he should come into a certain latitude, and at the peril of his life follow the orders therein set down. This was an air of grandeur like what princes practice to their admirals and generals.—It was punctually comply'd with by *Davis,* who read it to the ship's company; it contained no less than a generous deed of gift of the ship and cargo, to *Davis* and the crew, ordering him to go to *Brazil* and disposing of the lading to the best advantage, and to make a fair and equal dividend with the rest. *Davis* proposed to the crew, whether they were willing to follow their directions, but to his great surprise, found the majority of them altogether averse to it, wherefore in a rage, he bid them be damn'd, and go where they would. They knew that part of their cargo was consigned to certain merchants at *Barbadoes,* wherefore they steered for that island. When they arrived, they related to these merchants the unfortunate death of *Skinner,* and the proposal which had been made to them by *Davis*; upon which *Davis* was seized and committed to prison, where he was kept three months; however, as he had been in no act of piracy, he was discharged without being brought to any trial, yet he could not expect any employment there.

However, *Davis* was not long out of business. He found an employment on board a sloop, on which many of the hands on board were the pirates lately come in upon the late act of grace. The first place they touched at, was the island of *Martinico,* belonging to the *French,* where *Davis* having conspired with some others, rose in the night, secured the master and seized the sloop. A council of war was called over a large bowl of punch, at which it was proposed to choose a commander; the election was soon over, for it fell upon *Davis* by a great majority. Then he made a short speech, the sum of which was a declaration of war against the whole world. The first sail which fell in their way, was a *French* ship of twelve guns. He attacked this ship, and she soon struck. Soon a sail was spied a great way to windward of them. They enquired of the *French* man what she might be, he answered, that he had spoke with a great ship the day before. *Davis* proposed to attack her, but his men looked upon it to be an extravagant attempt, and discovered no fondness for it, but he assured them he had a stratagem in his head would make all safe; wherefore he gave chase, and ordered his *French* ship to do the same. The *French* ship being a slow sailor, *Davis* first came up with the enemy, and standing along side of them, showed his piratical colors: They, much surprised, called to *Davis,* telling him, they wondered at his impudence in venturing to come so near them. In the mean time the prize drew near, who obliged all the prisoners to come upon deck in white shirts, to make a show of force, as they had been directed by *Davis.* The shipmen were so intimidated by this appearance of force, that they struck. The *French* captain was in such a rage, at being so outwitted, that he was going to throw himself overboard, but was prevented by his men.

Having let go both his prizes, he steered northward. They met with a great many ships and vessels, all which they plundered, taking out of them whatever they wanted; and also strengthen'd themselves with a great many fresh hands, who most of them enter'd voluntarily. It was proposed what course they should steer, and differing in their opinions, they divided, and by a majority it was carry'd for *Gambia* on the coast of *Guiney*; of this opinion was *Davis,* he having been employed in that trade, was acquainted with the coast: He told them, that there was a great deal of money always kept in *Gambia Castle,* and that it would be worth their while to make an attempt upon it. They ask'd him how it was possible, since it was garrisoned? He desired they would leave the management of it to him, and he would undertake to make them masters of it. They began now to conceive so high an opinion of his conduct, as well as courage, that they thought nothing impossible to him, therefore they agreed to obey him, without enquiring further into his design. Having come within sight of the place, he ordered all his men under deck, except as many as were absolutely necessary for working the ship, that those from the fort seeing a ship with so few hands, might have no suspicion of her being any other than a trading vessel. Being come to the landing place, he was received by a file of musketeers, and

conducted into the fort, where the *Governor* accosting them civilly, ask'd them who they were, and whence they came? They answered they were of *Liverpool*, bound for the river of *Senegal* to trade for gum and elephants' teeth. The *Governor* asked them, if they had any *European* liquor on board? They answered a hamper should be at his service. The *Governor* then very civilly invited them all to stay and dine with him.

While he was in the fort, his eyes were very busy in observing how things lay. Now when *Davis* came back on board, he assured his men of success, desiring them not to get drunk, and that as soon as they saw the flag upon the castle struck, they might conclude he was master. He ordered his men, who were to go in the boat with him, to put two pair of pistols each under their clothes, he doing the like himself, and gave them directions to go into the guard room, and to enter into conversation with the soldiers, and observe when he should fire a pistol through the *Governor's* window, to start up at once, and secure the arms in the guard room. When *Davis* arrived, dinner not being ready, the *Governor* proposed that they should pass their time in making a bowl of punch till dinner time. *Davis* on a sudden drew out a pistol, clapped it to the *Governor's* breast, telling him, he must surrender the fort and all the riches in it or he was a dead man. The *Governor* being no ways prepared for such an attack, promised to be very passive, and do all they desired, therefore they shut the door, took down all the arms that hung in the hall, and loaded them. *Davis* fires his pistol through the window, upon which his men, without, executed their part of the scheme, like heroes, in an instant; getting betwixt the soldiers and their arms, all with their pistols cock'd in their hands, while one of them carry'd the arms out. When this was done, they locked the soldiers into the guard room, and kept guard without. In the mean time one of them struck the *Union Flag* on the top of the castle, at which signal those on board sent on shore a reinforcement of hands, and they got possession of the fort without the least hurry or confusion, or so much as a man lost of either side. *Davis* harangued the soldiers, upon which a great many of them took on with him.

This day was spent in a kind of rejoicing, the castle firing her guns to salute the ship, and the ship the castle; but the next day they minded their business, that is, they fell to plundering, but they found things fall vastly short of their expectation; for they discovered, that a great deal of money had been lately sent away; however, they met with the value of about 2000 pounds sterling in bar gold, and a great many other rich effects: Everything they liked, which was portable, they brought aboard their ship; and then they fell to work in dismounting the guns, and demolishing the fortifications.

After they had done as much mischief as they could, and were weighing anchor to be gone, they spied a ship bearing down upon them in full sail; they soon got their anchors up, and were in a readiness to receive her. This ship prov'd to be a *French* pirate of fourteen guns and sixty-four hands; the *Captain's* name was *la Bouche;* he expected no less than a rich prize, which made him so eager in the chase. Since there was no escaping, he resolved to do a bold and desperate action, which was to board *Davis.* As he was making towards her, for this purpose, he fired a gun, and hoisted his black colors; *Davis* returned the salute, and hoisted his black colors also. The *French* man was not a little pleased at this happy mistake; they both hoisted out their boats, and the *Captains* went to meet and congratulate one another with a flag of truce in their sterns; a great many civilities passed between them, and *la Bouche* desired *Davis*, that they might sail down the coast together, that he *(la Bouche)* might get a better ship: *Davis* agreed to it, and very courteously promised him the first ship he took, fit for his use, he would give him, as being desirous to encourage a willing brother. The first place they touch'd at was *Sierraleon*, where at first going in, they spied a tall ship at anchor; *Davis* being the best sailor first came up with her, and wondering that she did not try to make off, suspected her to be a ship of force. As soon as he came along side of her, she fired a whole broadside upon *Davis*, at the same time hoisted a black flag; *Davis* hoisted his black flag in like manner, and fired one gun to leeward. In fine she proved to be a pirate ship of twenty-four guns, commanded by one *Cocklyn*, who expecting these two would prove prizes, let them come in, least his getting under sail might frighten them away. This satisfaction was great on all sides, at this junction of confederates and brethren in iniquity; two days they spent in improving their acquaintance and friendship, the third day *Davis* and *Cocklyn* agreed to go in *la Bouche's* brigantine and attack the fort. The fort fired all their guns upon her, the brigantine did the like upon the fort, and so held each other at play for several hours, when the two confederate ships were come up to the assistance of the brigantine; those who defended the fort, seeing such a number of hands on board these ships, had not the courage to stand it any longer, but abandoning the fort, left it to the mercy of the pirates.

Having called a council of war, they agreed to sail down the coast together, and for the greater grandeur, appointed a commodore, which was *Davis;* but they had not kept company long, when drinking together on board of *Davis,* they had like to have fallen together by the ears, the strong liquor stirring up a spirit of discord among them, and they quarrell'd, but *Davis* put an end to it, by a short speech. Early in the morning, the man at the mast-head espied a sail. It must be observed, they keep a good lookout; for, according to their articles, he who first espies a sail, if she proves a prize, is entitled to the best pair of pistols on board, over and above his dividend, in which they take a singular pride. The ship proved to be a *Hollander,* and *Davis* putting out all his small sails, came up with her and fired a broadside; upon which she immediately struck, and called for quarters. It was granted, for according to *Davis's* articles, it was agreed, that quarters should be given whenever it was called for, upon pain of death. This ship proved a very rich prize, having the *Governor* of *Acra* on board, with all his effects, going to *Holland;* there was in money to the value of 15,000 pounds sterling, besides other valuable merchandises, all which they brought on board of themselves. As soon as he came in sight of the island, *High Cameroon,* he hoisted *English* colors; the *Portuguese* observing a large ship sailing towards them, sent out a little sloop to examine what she might be; this sloop hailing of *Davis,* he told them he was an *English* men of war, in quest of pirates. The *Portuguese* sent down a file of musketeers to receive him, and conduct him to the *Governor.* The *Governor* not in the least suspecting what he was, received him very civilly, promising to supply him with whatever the island afforded. Having cleaned his ship, and put all things in order, his thoughts now were turned upon the main business, viz. the plunder of the island, and not knowing where the treasure lay, a stratagem came into his head, to get it (as he thought) with little trouble. His scheme was to invite the *Governor,* with the chiefmen, and some of the friars, on board his ship, to an entertainment; the minute they came on board, they were to be secured in irons, and there kept till they should pay a ransom of 40,000 pound sterling. But this stratagem proved fatal to him, for a *Portuguese* swam ashore in the night, and discovered the whole plot to the *Governor.* However, the *Governor* dissembled, received the pirates' invitation civilly, and promised that he and the rest would go.

The next day *Davis* went on shore himself, as if it were out of great respect to bring the *Governor* on board: He was received with the usual civility, and he, and other principal pirates, who, by the way, had assumed the title of *Lords. Davis* and some of the *Lords* were desired to walk up to the *Governor's House,* to take some refreshment before they went on board; they accepted it without the least suspicion, but never returned again; for an ambuscade was laid, a signal being given, a whole volley was fired upon them; they every man dropp'd, except one, this one fled back, and escaped into the boat, and got on board the ship: *Davis* was shot through the bowels, yet he rose again, and made a weak effort to get away, but his strength soon forsook him, and he dropp'd down dead; just as he fell, he perceived he was follow'd, and drawing out his pistols, fired them at his pursuers: Thus like a game cock, giving a dying blow, that he might not fall unrevenged.

A flag from the frontispiece of *A General History of the Robberies & Murders of the Most notorious Pyrates,* 1724.

Captain BARTHOLOMEW ROBERTS

Bartholomew Roberts sailed in an honest employ from *London* aboard of the *Princess* of which ship he was second mate, and was taken in the said ship by *Captain Howel Davis. Davis* being cut off, the company found themselves under a necessity of filling up his post. Says one of them: *Should a Captain be so saucy as to exceed prescription at any time, why down with him! It will be caution after to his successors, of what fatal consequence any sort of assuming may be. However, it is my advice, that while we are sober, we pitch upon a man of courage, and skill'd in navigation, who seems best able to ward us from the dangers and tempests of an instable element. And such a one I take Roberts to be. A fellow! I think, in all respects, worthy your esteem and favour.* This speech was loudly applauded, and *Roberts* was accordingly elected; and he accepted of the honor, saying, that since he had dipp'd his hands in muddy water, and must be a pirate, it was better being a commander than a common man.

As soon as the government was settled, the company resolv'd to revenge *Captain Davis's* death. The pirates march'd in without opposition, set fire to the fort, and threw all the guns off the sea, which after they had done, they retreated quietly to their ship. *Roberts* put it to a vote of the company, whether their voyage should be to the *East-Indies*, or to *Brazil*; the latter being resolved on, they sailed accordingly, and in 28 days arrived upon this coast, where our rovers fell in, unexpectedly, with a fleet of 42 sail of *Portuguese* ships, off the bay of *los todos Santos*, with all their lading in, for *Lisbon*. *Roberts* mix'd with the fleet, and kept his men hid till they came close up to one of the deepest, and order'd her to send the master on board quietly, threat'ning to give them no quarters, if any resistance, or signal of distress was made. The *Portuguese* being surprised at these threats, and the sudden flourish of cutlashes from the pirates, submitted without a word, and the captain came on board. *Roberts* saluted him after a friendly manner, telling him, that they were gentlemen of fortune, but that their business with him, was only to be informed which was the richest ship in that fleet; and if he directed them right, he should be restored to his ship without molestation, otherwise he must expect immediate death. Whereupon this *Portuguese* master pointed to one of 40 guns and 150 men, a ship of greater force than the rover; but this no ways dismayed them, and so immediately steered away for him. When they came within hail, the master whom they had prisoner, was ordered to ask, how *Seignior Captain* did? and to invite him on board, for that he had a matter of consequence to impart to him; which being done, he returned for answer, that he would wait upon him presently. But by the bustle, that immediately followed, the pirates perceived they were discovered, and without further delay, they poured in a broadside, boarded and grappled her. The dispute was short and warm, wherein many of the *Portuguese* fell, and only two of the pirates. They found this ship exceeding rich, being loaden chiefly with sugar, skins, and tobacco, and in gold 90,000 *moidores* besides chains and trinkets, of considerable value; particularly a cross set with diamonds, designed for the *King* of *Portugal*.

Elated with this booty, they had nothing now to think of but some safe retreat, where they might give themselves up to all the pleasures that luxury and wantonness could bestow; and for the present pitched upon a place called the *Devil's Islands*, where they arrived and found the civilest reception imaginable, not only from the *Governor* and factory, but their wives. They then resolved one and all, to proceed for the *West-Indies*, where they took two sloops, and a few days afterwards, took a brigantine belonging to *Rhode Island*, and then proceeded to *Barbadoes*. Whereupon a galley that lay in the harbor was ordered to be fitted out with all imaginable expedition, and also a sloop. The *Barbadoes* ship kept an easy sail till the pirates came up with them, and then *Roberts* gave them a gun, expecting they would have immediately struck to his piratical flag, but instead thereof, he was forced to receive the fire of a broadside, so that an engagement ensued. But *Roberts* being hardly put to it, was obliged to crowd all the sail the sloop would bear to get off. At length by throwing over their guns, they got clear; but *Roberts* could never endure a *Barbadoes* man afterwards, and when any ship belonging to that island fell in his way, he was more particularly severe to them than others.

They then sailed for *Newfoundland*, and arrived upon the banks the latter end of June, 1720. They entered the harbor of *Trepassi*, with their black colors flying, drums beating and trumpets sounding. The vessels in the harbor all quitted upon sight of the pirate, and the men fled ashore. It is impossible particularly to recount the destruction and havoc they made here, burning and sinking all the shipping. *Roberts* met with 9 or 10 sail of *French* ships, all which he destroyed

I HAVE DIPPED MY HANDS IN MUDDY WATER & MUST BE A PIRATE... A MERRY LIFE & A SHORT ONE SHALL BE MY MOTTO.

WE'LL ALL GO MERRILY TO HELL TOGETHER...!

ABH AMH

Capt. BARTHO. ROBERTS & The Hoisting of JOLLY ROGER
(The Name They Gave Their BLACK FLAG.)

Irons '74

except one which they seiz'd, and carry'd off for their own use. This they christened the *Fortune*, and sailed away on another cruise, and took several prizes, out of which they had several passengers on board, who were used very roughly, in order to make them discover their money, threat'ning them every moment with death, if they did not resign everything up to them. They tore up the hatches and entered the holds like a parcel of furies, and with axes and cutlashes, cut and broke open all the bales, cases, and boxes, they could lay their hands on. All this was done with incessant cursing and swearing, more like fiends than men. They told that the *King* and *Parliament* might be damned with their acts of grace for them; neither would they go to *Hope-Point*, to be hang'd up a-sun drying, as *Kidd's* and *Braddish's* company were; but that if they should ever be over-power'd, they would set fire to the powder, with a pistol, and go all merrily to hell together. Two days afterwards, they took a *Virginia* man which they plundered and let go, and sailed for the *West-Indies* to meet with such ships as (they used in their mirth to say) were consigned to them, with supplies. They passed some time in their usual debaucheries, having taken a considerable quantity of rum and sugar, so that liquor was as plenty as water, and few there were, who denied themselves the immoderate use of it; nay, sobriety brought a man under a suspicion of being in a plot against the commonwealth, and in their sense, he was looked upon to be a villain that would not be drunk.

They proceeded for the coast of *Guiney*, where they thought to buy gold-dust very cheap. In their passage thither, they took numbers of ships of all nations, some of which they burnt or sunk, as the carriage or characters of the masters displeased them. The pirates were obliged to dispatch their business in haste, because they had intercepted a letter giving an account of the *Swallow* man of war pursuing them, which bore away to round *Cape Lopez*. *Roberts's* crew discerning their masts over the land, went down into the cabin, to acquaint him of it, he being then at breakfast on a savory dish of *Solomongundy*, and some of his own beer. He took no notice of it, but as the *Swallow* approached nigher, things appeared plainer, and some of them declared it to *Roberts*. Those *Roberts* swore at as cowards, who meant to dishearten the men, and hardly refrained from blows. What his own apprehensions were, till she hauled up her ports, and hoisted their proper colors, is uncertain. But then being perfectly convinced, he slipped his cable, got under sail, and ordered his men to arms, without any show of timidity, dropping a first rate oath, at the same time, resolved, like a gallant rogue, to get clear, or die.

Roberts made a gallant figure, at the time of the engagement, being dressed in a rich crimson damask wastcoat and breeches, a red feather in his hat, a gold chain round his neck, with a diamond cross hanging to it, a sword in his hand, and two pair of pistols hanging at the end of a silk sling, slung over his shoulders (according to the fashion of the pirates) and is said to have given his orders with boldness, and spirit. Coming close to the man of war, he received her fire, and then hoisted his black flag, and returned it, shooting away from her, with all the sail he could pack. He had perhaps finished the fight very desperately, if death, who took a swift passage in a grapeshot, had not interposed, and struck him directly on the throat. They presently threw him over-board, with his arms and ornaments on, according to the repeated request he made in his life-time.

Roberts could not plead want of employment, nor incapacity of getting his bread in an honest way, to favor so vile a change, nor was he so much a coward as to pretend it; but frankly own'd it was to get rid of the disagreeable superiority of some masters he was acquainted with, and the love of novelty and change, maritime peregrinations had accustom'd him to. *In an honest service,* says he, *there is low wages and hard labor; in this plenty and satiety, pleasure and ease, liberty and power; and who would not balance creditor on this side, when all the hazard that is run for it, at worst, is only a sour look or two at choking. No a merry life and a short one, shall be my motto.*

When *Roberts* was gone, their spirits sunk; and they had no way left, but to surrender and soon receive a final sentence. *To a trading nation, nothing can be so destructive as piracy, or call for more exemplary punishment; besides the national reflection it infers, it cuts off the returns of industry, and those plentiful importations that alone can make an island flourishing; and it is your aggravation, that ye have been the chiefs and rulers in these licentious and lawless practices. Ye, and each of you, are adjudged and sentenced, to be carry'd back to the place from whence ye came, from thence to the place of execution, without the gates of this castle, and there within the flood-marks, to be hanged by the neck till ye are dead. After this, ye, and each of you shall be taken down, and your bodies hanged in chains.*

Captain ENGLAND

Edward England went mate of a sloop that sail'd out of *Jamaica*, and was taken by a pirate, from whence *England* had the command of a sloop in the same laudable employment. *England* was one of these men, who seem'd to have such a share of reason, as should have taught him better things. He had a great deal of good nature, and would have been contented with less mischievous pranks, could his companions have been brought to the same temper. But he was generally over-ruled, and in that abominable society, he was obliged to be a partner in all their vile actions.

Captain England sail'd to the coast of *Africa*, and took the *Eagle*, the *Charlotte*, the *Sarah*, bound to *Virginia*; the *Bentworth*, the *Buck* sloop, bound to *Maryland*, the *Carteret*, the *Mercury*, the *Coward* galley, the *Elizabeth* and *Katherine* of *Barbados*, and sail'd down to *Whydah Road*, where they found another pirate, one *Captain la Bouche*, who getting thither before *England* arrived, had forestall'd the market, and greatly disappointed their brethren. When the pirates put it to a vote what voyage to take, the majority carrying it for the *East-Indies*, they shap'd their course accordingly, and arrived at *Madagascar*, the beginning of the year 1720. They stayed not long there, but after taking in water and provisions, sail'd for the coast of *Malabar*, having made a tour of half the globe, as the psalmist says of the devils, going about like roaring lions, seeking whom they might devour. They stayed not long here, but sailing to *Johanna*, they met 3 ships coming out of that harbor, one of which, after a desperate resistance, they took; the particulars of which is related in a letter by *Captain Mackray*, dated at *Bombay*, Nov. 16, 1720.

Not far from Madagascar, we found 14 pirates belonging to the Indian Queen, commanded by Capt. Oliver de la Bouche, and concluding it might be of great service to the East-Indian Company to destroy such a nest of rogues, were ready to sail when we discovered 2 pirate ships standing into the bay of Johanna. I got under sail, yet the others basely deserted us, and left us engaged with barbarous and inhuman enemies, with their black and bloody flags hanging over us, without the least appearance of escaping being cut to pieces. But God, in his good providence, determin'd otherwise; for notwithstanding their superiority, we engag'd them both about 3 hours, during which, the biggest received some shot betwixt wind and water, which made her keep off a little to stop her leaks. The other endeavoured all she could to board us, by rowing with her oars, but by good fortune we shot all her oars to pieces, which prevented them, and by consequence saved our lives. When the pirates came aboard, they cut 3 of our wounded men to pieces. I made what haste I could to the King's Town, almost dead, having been sorely wounded in the head by a musket ball. At this town I heard that the pirates had offered ten thousand dollars to the country people to bring me in, which many of them would have accepted, only they knew the King and all his chief people were in my interest. About 10 days after, hoping the malice of our enemies was nigh over, I obtained leave to go on board the pirates, and a promise of safety, several of the chief of them knew me. Notwithstanding their promise, some of them would have cut me to pieces, had it not been for the chief Captain, Edward England, and some others I knew. In the end I managed my tack so well, that they made me a present of the shattered ship, and with jury-masts, and such old sails as they left me, and passage of 48 days, I arrived here almost naked and starv'd, almost in despair of ever seeing land.

Captain Mackray certainly ran a great hazard, in going aboard the pirate, and began quickly to repent his credulity. *England* was enclined to favor *Captain Mackray*; but the pirates were so provok'd at the resistance he made against them, that he was afraid he should hardly be able to protect him; he therefore advised him to sooth up and manage the temper of *Captain Taylor*, a fellow of a most barbarous nature, who was become a great favorite amongst them, for no other reason than because he was a greater brute than the rest. *Mackray* did what he could to soften this beast, and ply'd him with warm punch; notwithstanding which, they were in a tumult whether they should make an end of him, or no, when an accident happened which turn'd to the favor of the poor captain; a fellow with a terrible pair of whiskers, and a wooden leg, being stuck round with pistols, comes swearing and vaporing upon the quarter-deck, and asks, in a damning manner, which was *Captain Mackray*. The Captain expected no less than that this fellow would be his executioner. But when he came near him, he took him by the hand, swearing damn him he was glad to see him; and show me the man, says he, that offers to hurt *Captain Mackray*, for I'll stand by him; and so with many oaths told him, he was an honest fellow, and that he had formerly sail'd with him.

Captain England having sided so much to *Captain Mackray's* interest, was marooned on the island of *Mauritius*. He made a little boat of staves and old pieces of deal, left there, and went over to *Madagascar*, where they he subsists at present. other gentlemen of the profession took a small vessel, which gave an account of *Captain Mackray*, who had orders to pursue and engage, wherever he met them. This put them in a tempest of passion: *A villain,* say they, *that we have treated so civilly, as to give him a ship, and now to be armed against us! He ought to be hanged!* *Captain Taylor* was now successor to *England,* and luckily as rogues could wish, they found a *Portuguese* ship, her masts lost, and so much disabled by a violent storm that she became a prize to the pirates, with very little or no resistance, and a glorious one indeed, that in the single article of diamonds, there was to the value of between three and four millions of dollars.

MARY READ

SHE FOUGHT HIM AT
SWORD & PISTOL,
& KILLED HIM
ON THE SPOT · 1720.

G.I.

MARY READ

Now we are to begin a history full of surprising turns and adventures. *Mary Read* was born in *England*; her mother was married young to a man who used the sea, who going a voyage soon after their marriage, left her with child, which child proved to be a boy. Whether the husband was cast away, or died in the voyage, *Mary Read* could not tell; but however, he never returned more. Nevertheless, the mother, who was young and airy, met with an accident which has often happened to women who are young, and do not take a great deal of care; which was, she soon proved with child again, without a husband to father it, but how, or by whom, none but herself could tell. Finding her burden grew, in order to conceal her shame, she takes formal leave of her husband's relations, giving out, that she went to live with some friends of her own in the country. Accordingly she went away, and carry'd with her her young son, at this time not a year old. Soon after her departure her son died, but Providence in return, was pleased to give her a girl in his room, of which she was safely delivered, in her retreat, and this was our *Mary Read*. Here the mother liv'd till what money she had was almost gone. Then she thought of returning to *London*, and considering that her husband's mother was in some circumstances, she did not doubt but to prevail upon her, to provide for the child, if she could but pass it upon her for the same, but the changing a girl into a boy, seem'd a difficult piece of work, and how to deceive an experienced old woman in such a point, was altogether as impossible. However, she ventured to dress it up as a boy, brought it to town, and presented it to her mother-in-law as her husband's son. The old woman would have taken it, to have bred it up, but the mother pretended it would break her heart, to part with it. So it was agreed betwixt them, that the child should live with the mother, and the supposed grandmother should allow a crown a week for its maintenance.

Thus the mother bred up her daughter as a boy. It happen'd that the grandmother died, by which means the subsistance that came from that quarter, ceas'd, and they were reduced in their circumstances. Being now 13 years of age, and growing bold and strong, and having also a roving mind, *Mary Read* enter'd herself on board a man-of-war, where she served some time, then quitted it, went over into *Flanders*, and carry'd arms in a regiment of foot. And tho' upon all actions, she behaved herself with a great deal of bravery, her comrade, happening to be a handsome young fellow, she falls in love with him, and from that time, grew a little more negligent in her duty so that it seems, *Mars* and *Venus* could not be served at the same time. Her comrade himself could not account for this strange alteration in her, but love is ingenious, and as they lay together in the same tent, she found a way of letting him discover her sex. He was much surprised at what he found out, and not a little pleased, so that he thought of nothing but gratifying his passions with very little ceremony. But he found himself strangely mistaken, for she proved very reserved and modest, and resisted all his temptations; that she quite changed his purpose, so far from thinking of making her his mistress, he now courted her for a wife. This was the utmost wish of her heart, and when the campaign was over, they were publicly married.

The story of two troopers marrying each other, made a great noise. The adventure of their love and marriage had gained them so much favor, that they easily obtained their discharge, and they immediately set up an eating-house, which was the *Sign of the Three Horse-Shoes*, near the castle of *Breda*, where they soon run into a good trade. But this happiness lasted not long, for the husband soon died, and the peace of *Ryswick* being concluded, the widow having little or no trade, she again assumes her man's apparel and takes on in a regiment of foot. Here she did not remain long, but ships herself on board of a vessel bound for the *West-Indies*. It happened this ship was taken by *English* pirates. It is true, she often declared, that the life of a pirate was what she always abhor'd, and went into it only upon compulsion, intending to quit it, whenever a fair opportunity should offer itself, yet some of the evidence against her, upon her trial was that in times of action, no person was more resolute or ready to board or undertake anything that was hazardous, than she and *Anne Bonny*; and particularly at the time they were attack'd and taken. When they come to close quarters, none kept the deck except *Mary Read* and *Anne Bonny*, and one more; upon which, she, *Mary Read*, called to those under deck, to come up and fight like men, and finding they did not stir, fired her arms down the hold amongst them, killing one, and wounding others.

In their cruise they took a great number of ships, and among these was a young fellow of a most engaging behavior, or, at least, he was so in the eyes of *Mary Read*. When she found he had a friendship for her, as a man, she suffered the discovery to be made, by carelessly showing her breasts, which were very white. Now begins the scene of love; as he had a liking and esteem for her, it was now turn'd into fondness and desire. Her passion was no less violent than his, and perhaps she express'd it by one of the most generous actions that ever Love inspired. It happened this young fellow had a quarrel with one of the pirates, and they had appointed to go ashore and fight. *Mary Read* was to the last degree uneasy and anxious, for the fate of her lover; she would not have had him refuse the challenge, because, she could not bear the thoughts of his being branded with cowardice. On the other side, she dreaded the event, and apprehended the fellow might be too hard for him. She took a resolution of quarrelling with this fellow herself, and having challenged him, she appointed the time two hours sooner than that when he was to meet her lover, where she fought him at sword and pistol, and killed him upon the spot. In fine, the lovers plighted their troth to each other, which *Mary Read* said, she look'd upon to be as good a marriage, in conscience, as if it had been done by a minister in church; and to this was owing her great belly, which she pleaded to save her life. Being found quick with child, her execution was respited, and it is possible she would have found favor, but she was seiz'd with a violent fever, soon after her trial, of which she died in prison.

ANNE BONNY

Anne Bonny was born in the kingdom of *Ireland*, her father an attorney at law; but she was not one of his legitimate issue. Having a great affection for the girl, which he had by his maid, he had a mind to take it home, to live with him. But to disguise the matter from his wife, he had it put into breeches, as a boy, pretending it was a relation's child he was to breed up to be his clerk. The wife enquired further, and talking with the child, found it to be a girl, and discovered that the servant-maid was its mother, and that the husband still kept up his correspondence with her. Upon this intelligence, the wife became unwilling to maintain bastards. The husband enraged, in a kind of revenge, takes the maid home, and lives with her publicly, to the great scandal of his neighbors. But he soon found the bad effect of it, for by degrees he lost his practice, so that he saw plainly he could not live there. Therefore he thought of removing, and with his maid and daughter embarks for *Carolina*. At first he followed the practice of the law in that province, but afterwards fell into merchandise, which proved more successful to him, for he gained by it sufficient to purchase a considerable plantation. His maid, who passed for his wife, happened to die, after which his daughter, our *Anne Bonny*, now grown up, kept his house.

She was of a fierce and courageous temper, wherefore, several stories were reported of her, as that she had kill'd an *English* servant-maid once in her passion with a case-knife. It was certain she was so robust, that once, when a young fellow would have lain with her, against her will, she beat him so, that he lay ill of it a considerable time. While she lived with her father, she was look'd upon as one that would be a good fortune, wherefore it was thought her father expected a good match for her; but she spoil'd all, for without his consent, she married a young fellow, who belong'd to the sea, and was not worth a groat; which provoked her father to such a degree, that he turn'd her out of doors, upon which the young fellow, who married her, finding himself disappointed in his expectation, shipped himself and wife, for the *Island of Providence*.

Here she became acquainted with *Rackam* the pirate, who making courtship to her, soon found means of withdrawing her affections from her husband, so that she consented to elope from him and go to sea with *Rackam* in men's clothes. And when any business was to be done, nobody was more forward or courageous than she, and particularly when they were taken. The day that *Rackam* was executed, he was admitted to her; but all the comfort she gave him, was, that she was sorry to see him there, but if he had fought like a man, he need not have been hang'd like a dog. She was continued in prison, to the time of her lying in, and afterwards reprieved from time to time; but what is become of her since, we cannot tell; but she was not executed.

Captain EDWARD LOW

Edward Low was born in *Westminster*, and had his education there. Nature seem'd to have designed him for a pirate from his childhood, for very early he began the trade of plundering, and was wont to raise contributions from the boys of *Westminster*. The virtues of some of his family were equal to his; one of his brothers was a youth of genius, when he was but seven years old, he used to be carry'd in a basket, upon a porter's back, into a crowd, and snatch hats and wigs. But to return to *Ned*, when he came to a man's estate, at his eldest brother's desire, he went to sea with him, and then work'd in a rigging-house in *Boston* in *New-England*, for a while. But being too apt to disagree with his masters, he left them, and shipp'd himself in a sloop that was bound to the *Bay of Honduras*.

The Captain being in a hurry provoked the boat's crew, but particularly *Low*, who takes up a loaded musket and fires at the Captain, but missing him, shot another poor fellow through the head, and with his twelve companions goes to sea. The next day they took a small vessel, and go in her, make a black flag, and declared war against all the world. They then proceeded to the *Island of the Grand Caimanes*, and falling in company with *George Lowther*, another pirate there who paying his compliments to *Low*, as great folks do to one another when they meet, and offering himself as an ally; *Low* accepted of the terms, and so the treaty was presently sign'd. They took a brigantine of *Boston*, bound thither from *St. Christophers*, at which time they parted and *Edward Low* went into the brigantine, with 44 others, who chose him their captain. *Captain Low* sailed for Purchase, (as they call it) towards *Marblehead*, into the harbor of *Port Rosemary*, and there found 13 ships, but none of force, at anchor, so they spread their black flag, and ran in among them; *Low* telling them they should have no quarters if they resisted. In the meantime they mann'd and arm'd their boat, and took possession of every one of them, plundered them of what they thought fit and converted one to their own use. Some time after this, they met with two sloops bound for *Boston*, but there happened to be an officer and some soldiers on board, who gave them a warm reception. They now steered for the *Leeward Islands*, but in their voyage met with such a hurricane of wind, that the like had not been known; the sea ran mountains high, and seemed to threaten them every moment with destruction; it was no time now to look out for plunder, but to save themselves, if possible, from perishing. All hands were continually employed night and day, for the waves went over them, so that they were forced to keep the pump constantly going, besides bailing with buckets; yet finding themselves not able to keep her free, and seeing the utmost danger before their eyes, they turn'd to the tackle, and hoisted out their provisions, and other heavy goods, and threw them overboard, with six of their guns, so that by lightening the vessel, she might rise to the top of the sea with the waves. By their throwing over-board the heavy goods, the vessel made considerable less water, and they could keep it under with the pump only, which gave them hopes and new life. After the storm *Low* got safe to a small island, one of the weathermost of the *Caribees*, and there fitted their vessels. The storm just spoken of, was found to have done incredible damage in those parts of the world. The town of *Port Royal* was overflowed, and above half destroy'd. A more melancholy sight was scarce ever seen when the water ebb'd away, all the streets being covered with ruins of houses, wrecks of vessels, and a great number of dead bodies. *Low* took several sail and threaten'd all with present death who resisted, which struck such a terror to them, that they yielded themselves up a prey to the villains, without firing a gun. They took a *French* ship, and condemned it to the flames with the cook, who, they said, being a greasy fellow, would fry well in the fire. The *Wright Galley* had the ill fortune to come in their way; and because at first they showed inclinations to defend themselves, the pirates cut and mangled them in a barbarous manner. A passenger, putting on a sorrowful countenance at what he saw acted, one of this vile crew attacked him upon the deck, saying, he did not like his looks, and thereupon gave him one blow across the belly with his cutlass, that cut out his bowels, and he fell down dead without speaking a word. At the same time another of these rogues cutting at a prisoner, missed his mark, and *Captain Low* standing in his way, very opportunely received the stroke upon his under jaw, which laid the teeth bare. Upon this the surgeon was called, who immediately stitched up the wound; but *Low* finding fault with the operation, the surgeon being tolerably drunk, as it was customary for every body to be, struck *Low* such a blow with his fist, that broke out all the stitches, and then bid him sew up his chops himself, and be damned; so that *Low* made a very pitiful figure for some time after.

They proceeded now to the *West-Indies*, but before they had gotten far on their voyage, they took a rich *Portuguese* ship; *Low* tortur'd several of the men, to make them declare where the money, (which he suppos'd they had on board) lay, and extorted by that means, a confession that the Captain had, during the chase, hung out of the cabin window, a bag with 11,000 *moidores*, of which, as soon as he was taken, he cut the rope, and let it drop into the sea. *Low*, upon hearing what a prize had escap'd him, rav'd like a fury, swore a thousand oaths, and ordered the Captain's lips to be cut off, which he broil'd before his face, and afterwards murdered him and all the crew. After this bloody action, they continued their course and made prizes of a snow from *New-York*, a sloop bound to *New-York*, and a pink, bound to *Boston*; which last they burnt, because of *Low's* irreconcilable aversion to *New-England* men. *Low* came off *South-Carolina*, and met with three good ships who all came out of *Carolina* together two days before; then they took a ship belonging to *New-England*; as *Low* let none of that country depart without some marks of his rage, he cut off the captain's ears, slit up his nose, and cut him in several places of his body. Two brigantines from *Carolina*, a sloop from *Virginia*, and a sloop from *Philadelphia*, fell a prey to these villains, upon this cruise.

It happened that at this time one of his Majesty's ships was upon a cruise, on this station, and got intelligence of some of the mischievous actions of this miscreant, who came in sight of the pirates by break of day. The man of war, which was called the *Greyhound*, was rather inferior in force to the pirates. The two sloops, one of them called the *Fancy*, commanded by *Low* himself, and the other the *Ranger*, both hoisted their piratical colors, and fired each a gun. But when the rogues found who they had to deal with, they edg'd away under the man-of-war's stern, and she standing after them, they made a running fight for about two hours. The fight raged with a brisk fire on both sides, till the *Ranger's* main-yard was shot down, and the man-of-war, pressing close upon the disabled sloop, *Low*, in the other, thought fit to bear away, and leave his consort a sacrifice to his enemy, who (seeing the cowardice and treachery of his commadore and leader, having 10 or 12 men killed and wounded, and that there was no possibility of escaping) called out for quarters, and surrender'd themselves to justice, which proved severe enough to them a-while afterwards. The conduct of *Low* was surprising in this adventure, because his reputed courage and boldness had, hitherto, so possess'd the minds of all people, that he became a terror, even to his own men. But his behavior throughout this whole action, showed him to be a base cowardly villain; for had *Low's* sloop fought half so briskly as the *Ranger* had done, (as they were under a solemn oath to do) the man-of-war, in my opinion, could never have hurt them. The man-of-war carry'd its prize into *Rhode Island*, to the great joy of the whole province, though it had been more complete if the great *Low* himself had grac'd the triumph. Twenty-five were found guilty, and executed the 19th of July, 1723, near *Newport*. This narrow escape of *Low* and his companions, one would have thought might have brought them to a little consideration of their black and horrid crimes. But alas they were dead to all goodness, and had not so much as one spark of virtue to stir them up to be thankful for such an eminent deliverance. But, instead thereof, they vented a million of oaths and curses upon the Captain of the *Greyhound*, vowing to execute vengeance upon all they should meet with afterwards, for the indignity he put upon them. The first prey they next met with was a small sloop belonging to *Nantucket*, a whale-fishing, the master of which the pirates cruelly whipp'd naked about the deck, making his torture their sport; after which they cut off his ears, and last of all shot him through the head. Some days after, *Low* took a fishing boat off of *Block Island*, but did not perpetrate so much cruelty to her, contenting himself with only cutting off the master's head. But after taking two whale boats near *Rhode Island*, he caused one of the masters' bodies to be ripp'd up, and his entrails to be taken out; and cut off the ears of the other, and made him eat them himself with pepper and salt; which hard injunction he comply'd with, without making a word. The latter end of July, 1723, *Low* took a large ship, called the *Merry Christmas*, and fitted her for a pirate, assumed the title of *Admiral*, and hoisted a black flag, with the figure of death in red, at the main-top-masthead, and took another voyage to the *Western Islands*. In January last (1724) *Low* took a ship called the *Squirrel*, but what became of him afterwards, I can't tell. The best information we could receive, would be, that he and all his crew were at the bottom of the sea.

A PARCEL of BRAVE FELLOWS...
NOT OUR BUSINESS TO STARVE OR BE MADE SLAVES.

CAPT. GEORGE LOWTHER &
TWELVE of HIS CREW MAKING THEIR ESCAPE
OUT of THE CABIN WINDOW.

Captain GEORGE LOWTHER

George Lowther sailed out of the *River of Thames* in one of the *Royal African Company's* ships, as second mate. In May, 1721, this ship came safe to her port in *Africa*; however, the captain took a pique against *Lowther*, who, losing his favor, found means to ingratiate himself into the good liking of the common sailors; insomuch, that when the captain ordered him to be punish'd, the men took up handspikes, and threat'ned to knock that man down, that offered to lay hold of the mate. This served but to widen the differences between him and the captain, and more firmly attach'd *Lowther* to the ship's company, which was ripe for any mischief.

Lowther and the common sailors grew insolent and bold, even refusing to obey when commanded to their duty by the captain and the chief mate. The captain seeing how things were carry'd, goes ashore early one morning to the governor, who believed *Lowther* was going a-pirating. *Lowther* confined the chief mate and put the ship in condition for sailing. In the afternoon they weigh'd anchor and when they came out to sea, *Lowther* call'd up all the company, and told them, it was the greatest folly imaginable to think of returning to *England*, for what they had already done could not be justified upon any pretense whatsoever, but would be look'd upon, in the eye of the law, a capital offence; that they had a good ship under them, and therefore, they should seek their fortunes upon the seas, as other adventurers had done before them.

Near *Barbadoes*, he came up with a brigantine, belonging to *Boston*, which they plundered in a piratical manner. They stayed some time at a small island to take their diversions, which consisted in unheard of debaucheries, with drinking, swearing, and rioting, in which there seemed to be a kind of emulation among them, resembling rather devils than men, striving who should outdo one another in new invented oaths and execrations. They met with a small vessel in the same honorable employment with themselves; the captain was one *Edward Low*. *Lowther* received them as friends, inviting them, as they were few in number, and in no condition to pursue the account, (as they called it) to join their strength together, which was accepted.

They took several vessels, viz. 2 brigantines of *Boston*; a sloop belonging to *Connecticut*; a sloop of *Jamaica, Captain Alexander Hamilton*; a sloop of *Virginia*; a sloop belonging to *Rhode Island*. With this little fleet, viz. *Admiral Lowther, Captain Low*, &c., the pirates came to the *Gulf of Martinique*, where of a sudden a considerable body of the natives attack'd them unprepared. As they were in no condition to defend themselves, they fled to their sloops, leaving their plunder, stores, &c., which was of great value. They then stood to the northward, intending to visit the main coast of *America*, and took a brigantine of *Boston*. At the taking of this vessel, the crews divided; for *Low*, proving always a very unruly member of the commonwealth, he thought it the safest way to get rid of him, upon any terms. They parted the bear skin between them; *Low* with forty-four hands, and *Lowther* with the same number.

It was now thought necessary to clean their sloop, and accordingly, *Lowther* unrigged, sent his guns, sails, rigging, &c. ashore, and put his vessel upon the careen. The *Eagle*, sloop of *Barbadoes*, belonging to the *South Sea Company*, coming near, saw the said sloop just careen'd, with her guns out, and sails unbent, which she supposed to be a pirate, because it was a place where traders did not commonly use, so took the advantage of attacking her, as she was unprepared. The *Eagle* engaged them till they called for quarters and struck, at which time *Lowther* and 12 of the crew made their escape out of the cabin window. The master of the *Eagle* went ashore in pursuit, but could find but 5 of them. The *Spanish* governor being informed of this brave action, sent a small sloop to scour for the pirates, and took 4 more, who were try'd and condemned to slavery for life. The *Eagle* sloop brought all their prisoners afterwards to *St. Christophers*, where they were found guilty and executed, March 20, 1724. As for *Captain Lowther*, it is said, that he afterwards shot himself, being found by some sloop's men, dead, and a pistol burst by his side.

HERE'S FOR BRINGING HORSES WITHOUT BOOTS & SPURS, FOR WANT of WHICH WE ARE NOT ABLE TO RIDE LIKE GENTLEMEN!

CAPT SPRIGGS TAKING A SHIP FROM RHODE ISLAND LOADEN WITH SOME HORSES

·1724·

When they fight under Jolly Roger they give quarter, which they do not when they fight under the red or bloody flag.
From Captain Hawkins' account of his capture by Captain Spriggs, 1724.

Captain FRANCIS SPRIGGS

Spriggs sailed with *Low* for a pretty while, when come away from *Lowther*. He was quartermaster to the company, and along with him had a great share in all the barbarities committed by that execrable gang. When *Low* took a ship on the coast of *Guiney*, *Spriggs* took possession of the ship with 18 men, left *Low* in the night, and came to the *West-Indies*. This separation was occasioned by a quarrel with *Low*, concerning a piece of justice *Spriggs* would have executed upon one of the crew, for killing a man in cold blood, as they call it, one insisting that he should be hang'd, and the other that he should not. A day or two after they parted, *Spriggs* was chose Captain by the rest, and a black ensign was made, which they called *Jolly Roger*, with the same device that *Captain Low* carry'd, viz. a white skeleton in the middle of it, with a dart in one hand striking a bleeding heart, and in the other, an hourglass; when this was finished and hoisted, they fired all their guns to salute their captain and themselves, and then looked out for prey. Near the island of *St. Lucia*, they took a sloop belonging to *Barbadoes*, which they plundered, and then burnt, forcing some of the men to sign their articles. The others they beat and cut in a barbarous manner because they refused to take on with the crew, and then sent them away in the boat, who all got safe afterwards to *Barbadoes*. The next was a *Martinico* man, which they served as bad as they had done the others. Some days afterwards, they took a ship coming from *Jamaica*. They took out her things, as they thought fit, and what they did not want, they threw overboard or destroy'd. They cut the cable to pieces, knocked down the cabins, broke all the windows, and in short took all the pains in the world to be mischievous. On the 27th they took a *Rhode Island* sloop, and all the men were obliged to go aboard the pirate. But the mate being a grave sober man, and not enclinable to stay, they told him, he should have his discharge, and that it should be immediately writ on his back; whereupon he was sentenced to receive ten lashes from every man in the ship, which was rigorously put in execution. The next day was spent in boysterous mirth, roaring and drinking of healths, among which was, by mistake, that of *King George the II*, for you must know, now and then the gentry are provok'd to sudden fits of loyalty, by the expectation of an act of grace.

Spriggs stood towards *Bermuda*, and took a scooner belonging to *Boston*; he took out all the men and sunk the vessel, and had the impudence to tell the masters, that he designed to encrease his company on the banks of *Newfoundland*, and then would sail for the coast of *New-England*. Windward of *St. Christophers*, on the 4th of June, 1724, they took a sloop belonging to *St. Eustatia*, and wanting a little diversion, they hoisted the men as high as the main- and fore-tops, and let them run down amain, enough to break all the bones in their skins, and after they had pretty well crippled them by this cruel usage, and by whipping them along the deck, they let them go, keeping back only 2 men, besides the plunder of this vessel. Within 2 or 3 days they took a ship coming from *Rhode Island* to *St. Christophers*, loaden with provisions and some horses; the pirates mounted the horses and rid them about the deck, backwards and forwards at full gallop, like madmen at *New-Market*, cursing, swearing, and hallowing at such a rate, that made the creatures wild. At length two or three of them throwing their riders, they fell upon the ship's crew, and whipp'd, cut, and beat them in a barbarous manner, telling them, it was for bringing horses without boots and spurs, for want of which they were not able to ride like gentlemen. About the beginning of the New Year [1725], they took a ship bound from *Jamaica* to *New-England*, which, after they had plunder'd, they were about to put all the negroes aboard that were taken in the above-mention'd sloop. But the captain representing his great want of provisions, and the danger of their perishing by famine, if he took them in, he was set at liberty upon his taking only ten of them, whom he carry'd to *South-Carolina*, whither he was forc'd to put in for a fresh supply of provisions. After this *Spriggs* met with *Capt. Durfy*, off *Rhode Island*, whom he plunder'd in the usual manner. *Spriggs* having got provisions and necessaries out of the vessels lately taken, he alter'd his voyage, because of the cold weather and hard gales of wind, and came into a warmer latitude. Off the west end of *Cuba Spriggs* was met with by a man of war, who chas'd them over to the *Florida* shore, where their sloop run aground and was lost.

GOOD DEVIL, TAKE THIS 'TILL I COME!

HONEST
CAPTAIN LEWIS
WHO AS A LUSTY LAD
HAD BEEN AN
EARLY PIRATE
c· 1670 - 1726

g.Irons·75·

Captain LEWIS

This worthy gentleman was an early pirate. We first find him a boy on board the pirate *Banister*, who was hang'd at the yard-arm of a man of war in sight of *Port-Royal*, in *Jamaica*. This *Lewis* and another boy were taken with him, and brought into the island hanging by the middle at the mizen-peek. He had a great aptitude for languages, and spoke perfectly well that of the *Mosquito Indians*, the *French*, *Spanish* and *English*. I mention our own, because it is doubted whether he was *French* or *English*, for we cannot trace him back to his original. He sailed out of *Jamaica* till he was a lusty lad, and was then taken by the *Spaniards* at the *Havana*, where he stayed some time. But at length he and six more ran away with a small canoe, and surprised a *Spanish* pettiauga, out of which two men joined them, so that they now were nine in company. With this pettiauga they surprised a turtling sloop, and forced some of the hands to take on with them, the others they sent away in the pettiauga. He play'd at this small game, surprising and taking coasters and turtlers, till with volunteers he made up a complement of 40 men.

With these he took a large ship, from *Jamaica*, and after her several others. And having intelligence of a fine brigantine, he sent the captain a letter, the purport of which was, that he wanted such a brigantine, and if he would part with her, he would pay him honestly 10,000 pieces of eight. If he refused this, he would take care to lie in his way, for he was resolved, either by fair or foul means, to have the vessel. The captain, having read the letter, sent for the masters of 10 *Bermudas* sloops lying there, and told them that if they would make up 54 men he would go out and fight the pirates. They said, no, they would not hazard their men, they depended on their sailing, and everyone must take care of himself as well as he could. However, they all put to sea together, and spied a sail under the land, which had a breeze while they lay becalmed. Some said he was a turtler, others, the pirate, and so it proved. For it was honest *Captain Lewis*, who putting out his oars, got in among them. The brigantine called to all the sloops to send him men, and he would fight *Lewis*, but to no purpose; nobody came on board him. In the mean while a breeze sprung up, and the brigantine left them, who all fell a prey to the pirate.

After these captures he cruised in the *Gulf of Florida*, lying in wait for the *West-India* homeward bound ships which took the leeward passage, several of which falling into his hands were plundered by him. From hence he went to the coast of *Carolina*, where the natives traded with him for rum and sugar, and brought him all he wanted, without the government's having any knowledge of him; for he had got into a very private creek. From *Carolina* he cruised on the coast of *Virginia*, where he took and plunder'd several merchant-men, and then return'd to the coast of *Carolina*, where he did abundance of mischief. From the coast of *Carolina* he shaped his course for the banks of *Newfoundland*, where he over-hauled several fishing vessels, and then went into a commodious harbor in *Conception Bay*, and seized a 24 gun galley, called the *Herman*. The commander told *Lewis*, if he would send his quarter-master ashore he would furnish him with necessaries. He being sent ashore, a council was held among the masters, the consequence of which was, the seizing the quarter-master, whom they carried to *Captain Woodes Rogers*. He chained him to a sheet anchor which was ashore. *Lewis*, swearing he would have his quarter-master, intercepted two fishing shallops, on board of one was the captain of the galley's brother. *Lewis* detained them, and sent word, if his quarter-master did not immediately come off, he would put all his prisoners to death. The quarter-master was sent on board him without hesitation. *Lewis* and the crew enquired how had he been used? and he answered, very civilly. *It's well*, said the pirate; *for had you been ill treated, I would have put all these rascals to the sword.*

From *Newfoundland* he steer'd for the coast of *Guiney*, where he took a great many ships, among which was one belonging to *Carolina*, commanded by *Captain Smith*. While he was in chase of this vessel an accident happen'd, which made his men believe he dealt with the *Devil*; for, he carried his fore- and main-top-mast, and running up the shrouds to the main-top, tore off a handful of hair, and throwing it into the air, used this expression, *Good Devil take this till I come*: And, it was observed, that he came afterwards faster up with the chase than before the loss of his top-masts. *Smith* being taken, *Lewis* used him very civilly, and gave him as much, or more in value, than he took from him, and let him go, saying, he would come to *Carolina* when he had made money on the coast, and would rely on his friendship. *Lewis* was informed the *French* in his crew had a plot against him. He answer'd, he could not withstand his destiny; for the *Devil* told him in the great cabin, he should be murdered that night. In the dead of night came the rest of the *French* on board in canoes, got into the cabin and killed *Lewis*.